School Leader Problem-Solving Skills

School Leader Problem-Solving Skills

Situational Judgment Tests from School Leaders

Wanda S. Maulding Green
and Edward E. Leonard

ROWMAN & LITTLEFIELD
Lanham • Boulder • New York • London

Published by Rowman & Littlefield
An imprint of The Rowman & Littlefield Publishing Group, Inc.
4501 Forbes Boulevard, Suite 200, Lanham, Maryland 20706
www.rowman.com

86-90 Paul Street, London EC2A 4NE

Copyright © 2023 by Wanda S. Maulding Green & Edward E. Leonard

All rights reserved. No part of this book may be reproduced in any form or by any electronic or mechanical means, including information storage and retrieval systems, without written permission from the publisher, except by a reviewer who may quote passages in a review.

British Library Cataloguing in Publication Information Available

Library of Congress Cataloging-in-Publication Data Available

ISBN: 978-1-4758-7195-1 (cloth : alk. paper)
ISBN: 978-1-4758-7196-8 (pbk. : alk. paper)
ISBN: 978-1-4758-7197-5 (ebook)

Contents

Preface	vii
About the Contributors	xi
Introduction: The Concept of Leader Acumen	xv
Chapter 1: Situational Judgment Tests	1
Chapter 2: Lessons on Credibility	3
Chapter 3: Lessons on Competence	15
Chapter 4: Lessons on Ability to Inspire	25
Chapter 5: Lessons on Vision	39
Chapter 6: Lessons on Emotional Intelligence/Soft Skills	51
Chapter 7: Contributing Authors' Solutions for Situational Judgment Tests	67
Appendix A: Small Group Cards	89
Appendix B: Leader Acumen Interpretation Matrix	91
Appendix C: Leadership Orientation	93
Appendix D: Fun at Work?	97
Appendix E: Self-Knowledge	99
Appendix F: Activities to Improve Your Leader Acumen	103
Notes	107

Preface

The world of PreK–12 education in the United States and worldwide, to state the obvious, has seen many dramatic changes since the previous publication of leadership situational judgment test scenarios four years ago. Nonetheless, after rereading the preface numerous times, we felt it still captured the essence of what we wanted to say with some additions based on current commentary and research. Those additions are addressed in the new portion of the preface contained in the fourth paragraph.

One of the key points about leader acumen is that the soft skills that comprise the major leader acumen imperatives of credibility, competence, inspirational ability, vision, and emotional intelligence/soft skills *can be learned*. Leaders, aspiring leaders, or anyone who wishes to build their leadership capacity, with proper exposure and practice, can learn new skills or enhance skills they already possess. Learning or enhancing skills builds a leader's adaptive capacity.

In *Geeks and Geezers: How Era, Values, and Defining Moments Shape Leaders*, Warren Bennis and Robert Thomas shared that,

> To the extent that any single quality determines success, that quality is adaptive capacity.... When we look at who becomes a leader, we see enormous variance in IQ, birth order, family wealth, family stability, level of education, ethnicity, race, and gender. Certainly, these factors cannot be dismissed entirely. But in studying both very young and older leaders, we found over and over again that much more important than a person's measured intelligence—to take just one factor—was his or her ability to transcend the limits that a particular IQ might impose. In the case of intelligence, this includes avoiding the trap of seeing oneself as highly intelligent, hopelessly average, or below average to the exclusion of other, more useful self-definitions. We emphatically agree with Ford's Elizabeth Kao that "everyone has their own wall to climb." And we believe that both the willingness to climb those walls and the ability to find ways to do so are the real measure of a leader.[1]

Bennis and Thomas go on to say that leaders "learn important lessons, including new skills that allow them to move on to new levels of achievement and new levels of learning. This ongoing process of challenge, adaptation, and learning prepares the individual for the next crucible, where the process is repeated. . . . Whenever significant new problems are encountered and dealt with adaptively, new levels of competence are achieved, better preparing the individual for the next challenge."[2]

Summarizing the concept of adaptive capacity in later writing, Bennis reemphasized the importance of adaptive capacity saying, "the ruling quality of leaders, adaptive capacity, is what allows true leaders to make the nimble decisions that bring success."[3]

Making correct decisions is based on three premises: knowledge of a given situation, technical (hard/competency-based) skills, and (soft) people skills. Knowledge of events will vary from situation to situation, but leaders cannot succeed without the people skills that allow them to fully utilize their technical skills.

It is the recognition of the importance of acquiring the technical and people skills and moving to acquire and/or enhance those skills as new discoveries or innovations occur or when new strategies develop that is the cornerstone of building leader acumen that allows a leader's adaptive capacity to flourish.

Commentary and research since 2019 continue to emphasize the importance of adaptive capacity or the ability to accommodate change whether individually or organizationally. Speaking to the rate of change in business both before and after the pandemic, Harrison held that "The rate of change was incredible before the pandemic, but the pandemic accelerated that rate beyond normalcy. Not only did leaders have to visualize their teams' success and make it happen, but they also had to remain flexible to meet the wide variety of emerging issues. This marked a new era for business—one in which adaptive capacity is critical for survival."[4]

Ramalingam et al. share that "Leaders must adapt and so must the organization they lead. The Covid-19 pandemic is constantly evolving, with leaders facing unpredictability, imperfect information, multiple unknowns, and the need to identify responses quickly—all while recognizing the multi-dimensional (health-related, economic, social, political, cultural) nature of the crisis."[5] They hold that:

Responding to the crisis requires adaptive leadership, which involves what we refer to as the 4 A's:

- Anticipation of likely future needs, trends and options.
- Articulation of these needs to build collective understanding and support for action.

- Adaptation so that there is continuous learning and the adjustment of responses as necessary.
- Accountability, including maximum transparency in decision making processes and openness to challenges and feedback.[6]

On this same idea, Shoemaker and Day share that adaptability is driven by four considerations:

- *Leadership commitment to vigilance*, as demonstrated by an openness to weak signals from diverse sources, while encouraging others in the organization to explore issues beyond their immediate domain and think outside the box. Vigilant leadership teams focus externally and nurture curiosity at all levels and across silos. They are consistently willing to play a long game strategy.
- *Investments in foresight* are often made through centralized foresight units for scanning and by using strategic dashboards to monitor relevant future scenarios. Leaders insist on a disciplined search for investment opportunities. In parallel, they orchestrate a flexible, real options portfolio of possible responses.
- *Strategy-making processes* that are flexible and adaptive, by adopting "outside-in" and "future-back" approaches. Outside-in thinking starts with how the outside world is changing and not with the current strategy or resources. Future-back thinking asks what it takes to win in the longer term and how to plant the necessary seeds now.
- *Coordination and accountability* for receiving and interpreting weak signals, supported by an organizational norm of sharing information readily across silos.[7]

Fernandez and Shaw state regarding college and university leadership that "those leaders with the flexibility and adaptive capacity to learn and evolve as a consequence of navigating a 'crisis,' will be able to respond more effectively and with less effort to future challenges."[8]

In like manner, the *Creating the Dream* organization states that "it's increasingly important for us to deliver holistic, resilient, equitable, and student-centric systems. This requires transitioning to an adaptive culture that focuses on long-term sustainability through the generation of alternate paths, ideas, modes of operating, and behavioral norms."[9]

Addressing parochial education, Goode et al. hold simply that "It is adaptive leadership that enables change to thrive."[10] Dunn, citing Australian elementary and secondary education, likewise held that, "Adaptive approaches are capable of dealing with complexity, unpredictability and change. These are all aspects educational leaders recognise are evident every day in their improvement work, well before COVID-19."[11]

Moreover, Dunn shared that, "Adaptive leaders seek to mobilise knowledge quickly, are responsive to contextual needs, and seek to empower their colleagues to act, even when the path is unclear, and the journey might be messy."[12]

Regarding instructional leadership, Nurabadi et al. posit that principals "are not expected to be perfect leaders but to be flexible leaders having adaptive capacity to learn and develop amidst prevailing crisis or pandemic."[13] These commentators and researchers come to the same conclusion as Bennis and Thomas: adaptive capacity is vital to individual and organizational success.

School Leader Problem-Solving Skills: Situational Judgment Tests from School Leaders takes the reader through a series of situational judgment test scenarios that address the soft people skill areas that lead to success. In that sense, this third volume is no different from the first two.

Volume 3 is once again based on the experience of practicing or recently retired PreK–12 educational leaders and reveals that while new issues have arisen, many of the issues that leaders have always faced remain to be dealt with. It also suggests clearly that a leader must exercise their leader acumen and adaptive capacity to make correct decisions.

Developing or enhancing your leader acumen and adaptive capacity and thereby your ability to make proper decisions is a foundational leadership ability. *School Leader Problem-Solving Skills: Situational Judgment Tests from School Leaders* takes you on a leadership development journey.

About the Contributors

Ms. Jennifer A. Leonard Box is an educational veteran with experience in the classroom and as a school counselor in both secondary and post-secondary levels. More importantly, she is the proud daughter of one of this book's authors, Dr. Ed Leonard.

Ms. Elizabeth Butler is currently an assistant principal at Pascagoula High School. She is a former English teacher and volleyball coach. Ms. Butler received her degrees from Mississippi Gulf Coast Community College, the University of South Alabama, and the University of Southern Mississippi.

Ms. Tammy Crosetti is a licensed professional administrator. Throughout her career, she has worked as a classroom teacher, a math curriculum specialist, an assistant principal, and as a lead principal for a seventh-grade to twelfth-grade school. She currently works for the Mississippi Department of Education as the Director of Secondary Curriculum and Instruction.

Ms. Babette Duty is the superintendent of Covington County School District where she graduated high school and has worked for over thirty years as an educator. Ms. Duty is a former middle school English teacher. She received her degrees from William Carey University.

Dr. Brian Finnigan is the director at Saraland Alternative Learning Center. He is a former assistant principal, AP chemistry teacher, and University of South Alabama research chemist. Dr. Finnigan received his degrees from the University of Bridgewater and the University of South Alabama.

Ms. Congetta Ward Gieger is currently an assistant principal at South Jones High School. She is a former history and science teacher. Ms. Gieger received her degrees from Jones College and the University of Southern Mississippi.

Ms. Eva Harvell is currently the director of technology for the Pascagoula-Gautier School District. She is a former elementary teacher and technology integration specialist. Ms. Harvell earned three degrees from the University of Southern Mississippi and William Carey University.

Dr. Jason Golden is currently the principal at Rosa A. Lott Middle School. He is a former science teacher and football coach. He received his degrees from the University of Alabama and the University of South Alabama.

Mr. Brent Harrison is currently the principal at Saraland High School in Saraland, Alabama. Mr. Harrison has spent the last twelve years as an administrator and was a history teacher and coach for six years previously. Mr. Harrison received a bachelor's degree from Troy University, master's degree from the University of Montevallo, education specialist degree from Troy University, and is currently pursuing a doctorate from the University of South Alabama.

Ms. Raina Holmes is currently the principal of Vancleave High School. She has served as an assistant principal, special education teacher, history teacher, and head girls basketball coach. She has received her degrees from Arkansas State University and the University of Southern Mississippi.

Dr. Valerie Johnson, NBCT, is currently the principal at Dunbar Magnet School of the Creative and Performing Arts. She is a former school counselor and music teacher. Dr. Johnson received her degrees from the University of South Alabama.

Dr. Angela McHenry is currently the principal at Clarkdale Elementary. She is a former middle school teacher and counselor. Dr. McHenry received her degrees from the University of Southern Mississippi and Mississippi State University.

Dr. Justin McNellage is currently an assistant principal at Spanish Fort High School (Go Toros). He was a former English teacher at Saraland High School. Dr. McNellage received degrees from the University of Mobile and the University of South Alabama.

Mrs. Shacora Moore is currently the principal of Northeast Lauderdale Middle School. She is a former National Board–certified English teacher. Mrs. Moore received her degrees from Tougaloo College, David Lipscomb University, and the University of Mississippi.

Mrs. Jorine Neal is currently the principal at Partnership Middle School at Mississippi State. She has over twenty years of experience in education. She is a former high school special education teacher and elementary teacher. Mrs. Neal received her degrees from the University of Florida, Florida International University, and Arkansas State University.

Dr. Phatasis O'Harroll currently serves as the curriculum director for the Vicksburg Warren School District. Her academic portfolio consists of degrees from the University of Southern Mississippi and Mississippi College. Dr. O'Harroll is a National Board–certified teacher.

Dr. Patti Permenter is currently a William Carey faculty member and associate director of the Program of Research and Evaluation of Public Schools. With twenty-eight years of kindergarten to twelfth-grade experience, Dr. Permenter enjoys working with university students and educators in the field, especially with strategic planning and school improvement.

Dr. Brandon Quinn is currently the superintendent of the Alcorn School District. He has served as a teacher assistant, special needs classroom teacher, coach, athletic director, assistant principal, and principal. Mr. Quinn earned his degrees from the University of Mississippi, Scranton University, and William Carey University.

Mr. Derek C. Read is currently director of Career Technical Education & Workforce Development for the Pascagoula Gautier School District. He is a former instructor, coach, and career technical education counselor. Mr. Read received his degrees from the University of Mobile, University of Southern Mississippi, and William Carey University.

Ms. Fanesha Watts Terrell is currently the assistant principal at Oak Grove Middle School. She is a former lead teacher, special education teacher, case manager for special services, and math teacher. She received her degrees from the University of Southern Mississippi and William Carey University.

Introduction

The Concept of Leader Acumen

Leader acumen is defined as "a construct that represents the level of leadership capacity an individual possesses at any given time. It addresses the leadership imperatives of credibility, competence, ability to inspire, vision, and emotional intelligence/soft skills."[1] Each of these leadership imperatives is subdivided into knowledge, skills, and dispositions as shown in the following table. Each of the imperative subscale items lend themselves to defining the major category.

CREDIBILITY In 500 feet, stay right	COMPETENCE Recalculating	INSPIRATION Satellite reception lost	VISION You have arrived at your destination	EMOTIONAL INTELLIGENCE Route guidance suggested
Ethics or Personal Accountability	Discernibility	Enthusiastic	Commitment	Resilience
Honesty	Perception	Energetic	Sense of Direction	Communication and Listening
Responsibility	Conflict Resolution Skills	Passionate	Professionalism	Happiness
Trust	Problem-Solving and Decision-Making Skills	Optimistic	Decisive	Personality Traits
Integrity	Relationship Building	Genuine	Work Ethic	Sense of Humor
Sincerity	Planning and Assessment and Evaluation	Courageous	Concern for the Future	Assertiveness
				Flexibility
				Empathy/Interpersonal Interactions

Source: Wanda M. Green and Edward E. Leonard, *The Soft Skills of Leadership: Navigating with Confidence and Humility*, second edition (Lanham, MD: Rowman & Littlefield, 2019).

The Soft Skills of Leadership: Navigating with Confidence and Humility, second edition,[2] is an assessment for individuals regarding the imperatives; this assessment is referred to as the Leader Acumen Assessment. It includes the subscale items listed in the table. Ideally, the best starting point for using this field book is to take the Leader Acumen Assessment, if you have not yet done so. The assessment is available free of charge online at https://www.leadershipimprinting.com/.

This is a self-assessment, and it is vitally important that you are absolutely candid in your responses. The results of the assessment will give you a snapshot of your leadership capacity. It is important for the test-taker to acknowledge, however, that the assessment is a fluid one. You may take it today after a great day at work and reveal a higher score than you might, for instance, if taken when you have had many difficult days as a leader.

For a broader look at your leadership capacity, the authors suggest that you conduct a 360-evaluation (alternately referred to as a CIRCLE assessment) by having people you work with, those who evaluate you, or those who work *for* you complete the survey. Conducting a 360-assessment to accompany your self-assessment will provide you with a measure of the match or congruence of your view of your leadership capacity with the view of others directly associated with you as a leader or aspiring leader.

You may do this by inquiring on the website via the "Contact Us" page at https://www.leadershipimprinting.com/. Based on the results of your self-assessment and/or your 360-assessment, you are ready to work through *Leader Acumen Problem-Solving Skills: Situational Judgment Tests from School Leaders*. However, taking the assessment is not required to make good use of the field book.

The scenarios provided in the field book are a source from which to develop insight into and familiarity with the real-life situations with which PreK–12 educational leaders or leaders in general deal. Most any of the events described in the field book could and do happen to any leader (perhaps in a slightly different context). Leaders share many commonalities in terms of the issues with which they must deal, especially the soft skill/people-related issues.

HOW TO USE THE FIELD BOOK INDIVIDUALLY

Use of the field book is straightforward and simple. There are forty-one scenarios based on the five constructs of Leader Acumen. All of the scenarios are PreK–12 education-based but are potentially adaptive to other leadership situations.

Select a scenario. Read the scenario carefully. Think about the situation described and the possible solutions. Jot down in the space provided the solution you think would lead to the best outcome for the scenario. Then jot down a rationale for your solution.

After you have completed this part of the activity, turn to the end of the chapter where the "Contributing Authors' Options" are located. Read the options carefully and choose a best response from those listed. (Note, each scenario lists a final option that is blank. If you believe your solution is better than those provided by the authors, you should pencil your solution in at this time.)

With your solution and rationale in hand and your choice from the "Contributing Authors' Options" list (or your own solution), turn to the section of the field book titled "Contributing Authors' Solutions" for situational judgment tests (SJTs) to reveal the authors' solution[3] to the SJT (these are listed by chapter and scenario). Compare your solution and rationale to the "Contributing Authors' Solutions."

Close alignment of your solution and rationale with that provided suggests a well-honed sense of analysis of the situation. It is important to realize, though, that while some solutions and the accompanying rationale are better than others, there is often more than one acceptable way to resolve an issue/situation.

As a last step to gain further insight, the authors encourage you to read the complementary reading from *The Soft Skills of Leadership: Navigating with Confidence and Humility*, second edition,[4] and the relevant, contemporary selected related readings listed at the end of each scenario. Follow this same cycle as you read/work through the field book.

HOW TO USE THE FIELD BOOK WITH GROUPS OR INSTRUCTIONALLY

Using the field book as an instructional tool follows the same general pattern as for individual use with some differences. Divide the class into small groups. Provide each group with the SJT scenario. Instruct the group members to read the scenario carefully, think about the situation described and the possible solutions, and jot down individually in the space provided how they would respond to the scenario. Then jot down a rationale for the solution.

After each individual has completed this part of the activity, the facilitator should direct the groups to the end of the chapter where the "Contributing Authors' Options" are located. Individually, again, the class members should choose a best response from those listed. (Note: Each scenario lists a final option that is blank. If the student believes their solution is better than those provided by the authors, they should pencil it in at this time.)

Next, time should be allowed within the small groups to share their choices and come to group consensus on the best solution. Time should also be allowed for discussion and dialogue regarding the rationale for the individual choices. (Prior to class, instructors should prepare answer sharing cards to be utilized for this part of the activity. See appendix A for an example.) After ample small group discussion time has been given, the instructor should ask the small groups to raise the card with the letter of the solution they have chosen.

The instructor should then guide the large group instruction regarding the choices the small groups have made with ensuing dialogue. All of this rich discourse is intended to help grow participants' "adaptive capacity" for leadership. Additionally, the instructor may choose to share the "Contributing Authors' Solutions" with rationale along with rationale for rejection of the other choices. Repeat the process for each SJT scenario.

Whether used individually or in a group setting, the use of SJTs adds an element of realism to the concepts presented. SJTs also allow the reader to utilize their analytic skills and judgment in synthesizing a solution and rationale. Each of these are needed in a leadership situation as any decision can and, in all likelihood, will be examined and criticized, and a leader must be able to defend their decisions.

An additional and equally helpful step is to require class members to select a mentor for the duration of the term. Prior to each face-to-face meeting, assign an SJT for review and discussion. Have individual members work through the SJT with the mentor. When the class reconvenes, move directly from review of the scenario to small group dialogue regarding mentor/mentee interaction/solution. After small group discussion, reveal answer choice options for consensus among the group.

Finally, to fully solidify the learning from the class, the complementary reading from *The Soft Skills of Leadership: Navigating with Confidence and Humility*, second edition,[5] is listed at the end. Additionally, relevant, contemporary selected related readings are presented at the end of each scenario to solidify the learning gained through practice. We have found that requiring the participants to prepare a reflective writing helps them to internalize the ideas and solutions and is fruitful toward the desired end-product of leadership growth.

HEADED IN THE RIGHT DIRECTION?

The conceptual model for *Leader Acumen* is a GPS. With that framework in mind, there are many "directions" you might take to get to a final destination. As such, you may review your Leader Acumen Assessment and determine to work on the area where your score was lowest. That is fine. For example, you might skip over to the chapter with vision-growing scenarios if that works best for you. The field book was designed for use individually if desired.

If you are an instructor working with a class, the quickest route to your destination might be to work through from the beginning to the end. On the other hand, you might want to vary the scenarios to accommodate everyone in your class, rather than going through each topic before moving to the next. For you, getting to your destination might include waypoints along the route.

For all, the main thing to remember is that there are many ways to get to a specific destination. There is more than one correct way to solve a problem, and the quickest route to a solution may not always be the wisest. As you work through the scenarios, you will gain confidence in your navigational skills and become a better leader along the way.

Chapter 1

Situational Judgment Tests

Situational judgment tests (SJTs) are assessments where the test taker is presented with a real or hypothetical situation and is then asked to select the most appropriate response to that scenario. SJTs have been around since the early 1920s. They have been used for garnering feedback of those from managerial positions in the workplace to decision making ability in the military.[1]

Over the years, they have proved to be good predictors of job performance. The authors believe SJTs are a good tool to use, especially for a book of the nature of this one because, as McDaniel et al. put it, SJTs have:

- low adverse impact
- assess soft skills
- have good acceptance by applicants
- assess job-related skills not tapped by other measures, and
- assess "non-academic, practical intelligence."[2]

With those considerations in mind, the SJT is an excellent tool to use when growing one's skillset in leader acumen. As stated, the typical format of an SJT is for a brief scenario to be shared with the learner. Of course, this sharing may be done via video clip, live via role-play, or in a written form.

After the student acknowledges the situation, typically, they are given multiple choice responses to review and then select from. In this book, an additional step is added. Prior to exposure to the contributing authors' multiple-choice answer options, the student is allowed to pen their own brief response to the scenario.

This is done to allow the opportunity for rapid processing of *typical* thought processes: "What would I do in this situation without suggestion from others?" It allows the reader to reflect on their own "gut-level" response before being guided. This step, the internalization of an individual's usual/typical response, is critical in the growth aspect of this learning process.

It is important, then, for the reader to respond in the provided space as quickly and as honestly as possible. The reader should not be asking "how *should* I respond" but rather "how have I responded to a similar problem in the past" or even "what do I think is the best way to respond?"

For the classroom teacher, instructor, or workshop facilitator, SJTs have the best outcomes when the situation is presented to an individual (or group of individuals) via "live" mechanisms (i.e., role-play, video cast, or podcast). However, they are still effective when shared only in written form.

Traditionally, SJTs come in a variety of formats and responding mechanisms. Some are developed requiring the participants to rank-order the stated options, others ask the participants to give only the *best* answer, and yet others call for the *unacceptable* responses. For the most part, the SJTs included in this book ask for the participant to give the best response.

Additionally, the contributing authors have (at the end of the book) given the "Contributing Authors' Solutions" to the SJTs (whether correct or incorrect), a best response with a rationale for that decision, and, similarly, have given rationales for the other choice options. The most important take-away for these exercises is to help the reader hear a range of potential responses to a situation and, most importantly, for the participants, over time, to become reflective learners.

The richness of these assessments comes from the facilitation of an invested leader into and through individual, small group, and large group sharing and interaction. It is through these mechanisms that the best and most rapid learning can take place. Supporting readings from the companion book, *The Soft Skills of Leadership: Navigating with Confidence and Humility*, second edition,[3] follow each scenario but should not preempt the SJT itself. Additionally, selected relevant, contemporary related readings are presented at the end of each scenario to solidify the learning gained through practice.

SJTs were selected as the primary tool to help a student grow their own leader acumen. These learnings, as shared in *The Soft Skills of Leadership: Navigating with Confidence and Humility*, second edition,[4] take time and repetitive activity to establish as norms, as they are acquired in the most basal or primary parts of our brains.

Chapter 2

Lessons on Credibility

One of the things that people notice about a leader, possibly more than any other thing a leader does, is the extent to which their actions are consistent with their articulated position. Followers are asking and answering (to their own satisfaction) a vital question about the leader. Do they say what they mean and support that with their actions? The answer to that question defines the credibility of the leader.

The scenarios in this chapter are, in one way or another, related to a leader's credibility. If your Leader Acumen Assessment scores indicated this as an area for needed growth, you should work through the scenarios with a couple of things in mind. First, as you work through the scenarios in the chapter take particular note of the "Contributing Authors' Options" to each problem at the end of each chapter of situational judgment tests.

In working through the scenarios and reviewing the "Contributing Authors' Options," one of two things will happen. You will find disparity between your responses and the authors, or you might, indeed, find that your responses coincide with the authors' (see appendix B for a graphic representation). Next, reflect on the information you gained from the Leader Acumen Assessment. If you acknowledge that credibility is an area for growth based on the assessment, ask yourself if this was based on your self-assessment, the CIRCLE assessment, or both.

If either or both assessments (the self or CIRCLE) indicate that you have room for improvement in the area of leader credibility *and* you are also finding disparity in yours and the "Contributing Authors' Options," chances are you will find growth via working through these exercises and accompanying readings. However, be reminded that this will not happen overnight.

Growing your leader acumen is a worthy endeavor but is a painstakingly time-consuming undertaking. It requires rewiring of your thought processes regarding learnings that are very ingrained in your most innate understandings, and this takes time. (See appendix B for a graphic representation.)

On the other hand, if you find your solutions and the solutions offered in the "Contributing Authors' Options" coincide highly, yet your self score is lower than the means for the group shown at the end of your assessment for credibility, one of two things is happening. Either you are lacking in self-confidence, yet your decision making is solid, or conversely, perhaps you are somewhat overconfident, but nonetheless making good decisions.

If the first is the case, working through the scenarios should enhance your self-confidence. The second option (overconfidence) is the one to be most wary of. Leaders in this category often find themselves derailed as leaders, even though they generally are good decision makers. Working through the scenarios should help to instill the idea that there is more than one acceptable solution to most problems/issues and thus lessen one potential major consequence of overconfidence, feeling that you have the only viable solution.

If you opt to have a CIRCLE/360-assessment done and find that your solutions and the solutions offered in the "Contributing Authors' Options" coincide highly, yet your CIRCLE scores were outside the standard deviation (available from the Leader Acumen Team when a Circle/360-assessment is done) for credibility, it is possible that a different set of problems is occurring.

Either you are selecting the course of action you believe is best for the scenario, yet in reality you would not implement it, *or* the problem may be one of perception. It is much more likely that it is the former. Only in rare instances would the latter be the case. However, we insert it here for thought because, on occasion, it is the case. And, as the old saying goes: perception is reality.

Perhaps you are indeed highly credible, yet CIRCLE *perception* is the issue for your low scores in credibility. This could be a case of projection. For example, you may not "look" credible and perhaps for legitimate reasons. You will recall from the chapter on credibility in *The Soft Skills of Leadership: Navigating with Confidence and Humility*, second edition,[1] that mention was made of how "what you wear" infers or projects an image. Such could be the case in this instance.

Finally, improving your leader acumen and "adaptive capacity," as stated in the preface, is a process. As you will recall, the notion of leader acumen is predicated on the theory that there is a genetic predisposition toward leadership.

As Marquis and Tilcsik[2] so aptly noted, imprinting may take place during brief sensitive periods of high susceptibility during the formative process, during the teachable moment, or another yet different time of susceptibility, and that imprints once established are persistent.

The lessons in this book are to be utilized to grow leader acumen in this third way—over the long, repetitive process. To that end and to truly be imprinted with any of the competencies, actions for building the various skillsets may be found in appendix F.

True credibility is only gained by congruence of words and actions.

CREDIBILITY SITUATIONAL JUDGMENT TESTS

Snacks, Anyone?

One of the things students look forward to during break is purchasing snacks from the snack cart, which is sponsored by the Business Academy. On one particular day, I, as lead principal, decided to make a purchase from the cart; however, I didn't have money with me so I asked the sponsor to drop by my office after break to be paid. Later during the day, Mr. Smith came to my office to retrieve the payment.

I asked if he would be able to break a twenty dollar bill, to which he responded he could, and he proceeded to pull from his pocket about a five-inch roll of cash. Trying hard to keep my composure I managed to get out, "What are you doing carrying that much cash around?" He replied, "Oh, I always keep the money from the sales because when I need to buy items for the snack cart I don't have to go through the bookkeeper."

What do you do?

_____
_____
_____

SUGGESTED READING: Maulding Green, W., and Leonard, E. *The Soft Skills of Leadership: Navigating with Confidence and Humility*, second edition. Lanham, MD: Rowman & Littlefield, 2019, chapter 3.

ADDITIONAL SELECTED READINGS: Cooper, D. J., Hamman, J. R., and Weber, R. A. "Fool Me Once: An Experiment on Credibility and Leadership." *Economic Journal* 130, no. 631 (2020): 2105–33.

Mad Texting

Three female students were discovered to have made threats of violence toward each other on social media. These threats were made when the students were off campus. The threats were related to a fight that occurred over the weekend. The students specified that upon returning to campus, they would physically harm each other.

What do you do?

_____

Chapter 2

SUGGESTED READING: Maulding Green, W., and Leonard, E. *The Soft Skills of Leadership: Navigating with Confidence and Humility*, second edition. Lanham, MD: Rowman & Littlefield, 2019, chapter 3.

ADDITIONAL SELECTED READINGS: Jakobsen, F., Leth, M., Andersen, L., and van Luttervelt, M. "Theorizing Leadership Credibility: The Concept and Causes of the Perceived Credibility of Leadership Initiatives." *Perspectives on Public Management & Governance* 5, no. 3 (2022): 243–54.

Peek-A-Boo

A student walked away from a teacher while the teacher was giving the student instruction. The student was then brought to a school administrator, and the administrator assigned the student three days of in-school suspension. The student told the administrator that she would not go to in-school suspension and walked out of the administrator's office.

After about an hour, the administrator was able to locate the student in a bathroom. The administrator asked the student to come out of the bathroom, which she initially refused to do. However, after about ten minutes the student emerged. During this time, the administrator gave the student an ultimatum, "If you do not come out of the bathroom now, you will be assigned to forty-five days at the alternative school when you do come out."

What do you do?

SUGGESTED READING: Maulding Green, W., and Leonard, E. *The Soft Skills of Leadership: Navigating with Confidence and Humility*, second edition. Lanham, MD: Rowman & Littlefield, 2019, chapter 3.

ADDITIONAL SELECTED READINGS: Holdo, M. "How Can We Trust a Political Leader? Ethics, Institutions, and Relational Theory." *International Political Science Review* 43, no. 2 (2022): 226–39.

The Oversharing Employee

Over the holiday break, your district receives some severe weather damage. The district's maintenance department assesses the damage and begins to make the needed repairs for the school to open quickly.

The next day, you notice a Facebook friend has shared a video of the damage inside the school. After some investigation, you determine the video was taken by one of your classified employees. The video has been shared nearly one hundred times. The video does not violate the district's Acceptable Use Policy. However, the video is causing community concern and frustration about school opening back up too quickly and the competence of the maintenance department. The employee also put herself at risk by walking through the damage.

What do you do?

_____
_____
_____
_____

SUGGESTED READING: Maulding Green, W., and Leonard, E. *The Soft Skills of Leadership: Navigating with Confidence and Humility*, second edition. Lanham, MD: Rowman & Littlefield, 2019, chapter 3.

ADDITIONAL SELECTED READINGS: Zheng, Y., Graham, L., Epitropaki, O., and Snape, E. "Service Leadership, Work Engagement, and Service Performance: The Moderating Role of Leader Skills." *Group & Organization Management* 45, no. 1 (2020): 43–74.

Upgrade Complaints

The school district is upgrading the computers in the district, so the technology department has been in your building more than usual the last few weeks. One of your veteran teachers sends an email to you, complaining about how one of the technicians was rude to her while working in her room. This is not the first time the teacher has complained about a district employee being rude to her. No other teachers have complained about this particular technician.

What do you do?

_____
_____
_____
_____

SUGGESTED READING: Maulding Green, W., and Leonard, E. *The Soft Skills of Leadership: Navigating with Confidence and Humility*, second edition. Lanham, MD: Rowman & Littlefield, 2019, chapter 3.

ADDITIONAL SELECTED READINGS: Flowers, D. "Credibility in Times of Crisis." *Journal of AHIMA* 91, no. 4 (2020): 14–17.

Sticky Situation

An online student–teacher information system contains a lot of essential information regarding grades, attendance, addresses, parent contacts, and additional personal information. Teachers and administrators use this system daily to input and access student's school records.

A high school teacher had the password to her online student–teacher information system written on a sticky note attached to the bottom of her computer screen. It was spotted by a student who memorized the login code and began logging in from his own computer. The student began changing grades for himself and sharing personal information with other students.

A student from another class saw him access the system on his personal computer and, having concerns, notified the administration. When addressed, the student claimed the teacher gave him the password and allowed him to look at her account. The administrator then spoke with the teacher who shared that her password was on a sticky note and the student must have seen it when he stood near or around her desk. When the parent was informed, the parent blamed the teacher for having made her password accessible.

How do you handle the teacher?

_____
_____
_____
_____

SUGGESTED READING: Maulding Green, W., and Leonard, E. *The Soft Skills of Leadership: Navigating with Confidence and Humility*, second edition. Lanham, MD: Rowman & Littlefield, 2019, chapter 3.

ADDITIONAL SELECTED READINGS: Ziya, E., Epitropaki, O., Zhou, Q., and Graham, L. "Leader and Organizational Behavioral Integrity and Follower Behavioral Outcomes: The Role of Identification Processes." *Journal of Business Ethics* 176, no. 4 (2022): 741–60.

Duck, Duck, Goose

As a school administrator, it is imperative to be consistent. Even when the issuance of discipline is difficult due to the child or the circumstance, it is your job to enforce the rules. Unfortunately, when teachers do things to complicate situations, it sometimes results in second-guessing decisions made.

Matthew was an exceptional student. He had excellent grades, was always respectful, led the student section, and held multiple leadership positions in clubs on our campus. While he wasn't perfect, his teachers would often brag about him. At one point, a teacher shared that he was her favorite student because he was always nice and participated in classroom discussions.

One morning during this student's senior year, a teacher texted the administrators to come out to the student parking lot. The school administrators responded immediately. The teacher stated he found a shotgun in a student's vehicle. We asked the teacher several questions, and as it turned out, the teacher was told by a student. The teacher then took it upon himself to look in the toolbox in the student's vehicle. He stated that he wasn't sure what to do and he didn't want to bother administration if it turned out to be nothing.

The student was brought to the parking lot and his vehicle searched. Multiple guns, ammunition, and several knives were found. The student broke down and said that he knew about the knives, but he completely forgot to take out the weapons and ammo. He said that he and his buddies went duck hunting the weekend before, and it slipped his mind.

The student handbook lists firearms on campus as an expellable offense. There have been other instances, although different in nature, which have resulted in the expulsion of students.

What do you do?

_____
_____
_____
_____

SUGGESTED READING: Maulding Green, W., and Leonard, E. *The Soft Skills of Leadership: Navigating with Confidence and Humility*, second edition. Lanham, MD: Rowman & Littlefield, 2019, chapter 3.

ADDITIONAL SELECTED READINGS: Williams, R., Raffo, D., and Clark, W. "A Systematic Review of Leader Credibility: Its Murky Framework Needs Clarity." *Manag Rev Q* (2022).

Graduation Is Finally Here

Graduation is a momentous occasion that enables a school community to celebrate the milestone of students' achievements. For many students, graduation is a family tradition and an experience parents anticipate. For others, they are the first in their families to graduate high school, and the pressure of being a change agent in their families consumes them. As a school administrator, you and your administrative team are expected to plan and conduct a prestigious graduation ceremony that follows the school district's policy while allowing parents and students to celebrate the joys of graduation.

Jackson is an honor roll student, track star, and graduating senior at CountrySide High School who anticipates becoming the first child in his family to graduate from high school. Several local colleges are inquiring about Jackson's plans after graduation. The month before Jackson's graduation, he is involved in a verbal altercation resulting in a firearm being discovered on CountySide's campus.

Although Jackson did not own the gun, he was seen on camera near the vehicle where Jackson's friend stored the weapon. Before retrieving the firearm from the car, CountrySide's school resource officer confronted the teens in the parking lot. As a result of Jackson's involvement, you and your administrative team recommended him to the district's alternative school, where he will serve forty-five days pending a thirty-day review.

Jackson's mother does not challenge the school's decision. She requested that Jackson participate in the graduation ceremony, stating that as a first-generation high school graduate, his participation in the ceremony is significant to his family. She also stresses that Jackson is an honor student with no prior discipline issues. Jackson's alternative placement will end the day after graduation.

What would you do?

_____
_____
_____
_____

SUGGESTED READING: Maulding Green, W., and Leonard, E. *The Soft Skills of Leadership: Navigating with Confidence and Humility*, second edition. Lanham, MD: Rowman & Littlefield, 2019, chapter 3.

ADDITIONAL SELECTED READINGS: Jakobsen, F., Leth, M., Andersen, L., and van Luttervelt, M. "Theorizing Leadership Credibility: The Concept and Causes of the Perceived Credibility of Leadership Initiatives." *Perspectives on Public Management & Governance* 5, no. 3 (2022): 243–54.

Rigor or Relationships

School district policies are necessary but are not always clear and easy to follow. School leaders (and employees) must have working guidelines to follow, including checks and balances to stay out of legal trouble, and rules that create consistency across the district. The truth is, most policies are already set by the state, but there are a few policies that local school boards can create and/or change.

When attempting to change local policy, it is best practice to include all stakeholders by creating parent surveys, hosting community meetings, and receiving school board member feedback before ever placing the new policy in front of the board for approval. All this effort, though necessary, may be with little participation or concern. That is, until the policy change directly affects an individual parent or student once approved by the board.

Trey is a school employee at one of the local high schools and has asked for a meeting with you (as superintendent) in December, concerning his child who is a senior regarding the school district valedictorian policy. Trey has been an employee of the district for twenty years and a friend of your family for a lifetime. You happily grant Trey and his wife a meeting.

However, upon their arrival, you cannot help but notice that the tone of voice and body expressions appear anything but friendly. Trey starts the meeting by saying, "First of all, I am here as a parent not as an employee. I want that to be stated on the record." He then proceeds by explaining that his son has a 3.9 GPA and has been ranked first in his class but is ineligible to be valedictorian because of the policy that is in place.

Trey's son Thomas is an excellent student, athlete, and just a well-rounded young man. The current school board policy is that the valedictorian must not only have the highest GPA but must also be college and career ready per their ACT scores in English language arts and mathematics, as required for a distinguished graduate in the state. This policy was changed two years prior during Thomas's tenth-grade year.

The policy change was made to increase the rigor for all students in the district who sought to be valedictorian. Thomas's GPA and ACT–English language arts score met the requirement, but he was two points short on his mathematics score. Trey, as a lifelong friend, is simply asking that you as the school district leader modify the policy so that his son could be considered for valedictorian.

What do you do?

_____
_____
_____
_____

SUGGESTED READING: Maulding Green, W., and Leonard, E. *The Soft Skills of Leadership: Navigating with Confidence and Humility*, second edition. Lanham, MD: Rowman & Littlefield, 2019, chapter 3.

ADDITIONAL SELECTED READINGS: Ouedraogo, N., Zaitouni, M., and Ouakouak, M. L. "Leadership Credibility and Change Success: Mediating Role of Commitment to Change." *International Journal of Productivity & Performance Management* 72, no. 1 (2023): 47–65.

CONTRIBUTING AUTHORS' OPTIONS FOR CREDIBILITY SITUATIONAL JUDGMENT TESTS

Snacks, Anyone?

A. Tell him to be careful and make sure he doesn't leave it laying around where students could take the money.
B. Inform him of the district and school policy about all money collected.
C. Turn a blind eye and pretend you didn't see anything.
D. Reprimand the teacher for not following the school and district policy concerning collection of money.
E. Other option: _____

Mad Texting

A. Notify the parent(s) of the incident and warn them that if any future threats are made, the students will be suspended from school.
B. Verbally reprimand the students and escort them back to class.
C. Interview the students, determine if any others are involved, then suspend the students for a period as prescribed by district policy.
D. Send the student to the systems' alternative school for a period prescribed by policy.
E. Send the student to in-school suspension for a period as prescribed by policy.
F. Notify the police of the online threats.
G. Other option: _____

Peek-a-Boo

A. Notify the parent(s) of the incident and warn them that any future incidents of defiance the student will be suspended from school.
B. Verbally reprimand the student.
C. Interview the student to understand her actions.
D. Send the student to the systems' alternative school for forty-five days.
E. Send the student to in-school suspension for five days.
F. Suspend the student for five days.
G. Other option: _____

The Oversharing Employee

A. You do not take any action.
B. You ask the employee to delete the post from her Facebook page.
C. You address the employee regarding being on campus after her scheduled time.
D. Both B and C.
E. Other option: _____

Upgrade Complaints

A. You do nothing. The technician probably didn't do anything wrong.
B. You ask for written statements from both employees and have a conversation with the technology director about next steps.
C. You write the technician up for being rude to one of your employees.
D. You ask the technology director to assign the technician to another school.
E. Other option: _____

Sticky Situation

A. Discipline the student per handbook policy informing the parent of the consequences, but just have a discussion with the teacher.
B. Have a discussion regarding the seriousness of the offense with both the student and the teacher and inform the parent of the incident.
C. Discipline the teacher according to Code of Ethics and AUP Violation and discipline the student according to handbook policy, notifying the parent of the student's consequence.
D. Suspend the student's access to the internet for the remainder of the school year.
E. Other option: _____

Duck, Duck, Goose

A. Call the student's parents to remove the weapons from the vehicle and promise to monitor their student's actions more closely in the future.
B. Suspend the student for five days since he did not intend to use the firearms for malicious behaviors.
C. Send the student home immediately to put the weapons up and revoke his parking pass to avoid this from happening in the future.
D. Expel the student.
E. Other option: _____

Graduation Is Finally Here!

A. Tell Jackson's mother that because of his involvement in the situation he is not allowed to participate in the graduation ceremony because his actions put others in danger. Inform her that you will mail his diploma to his home address.
B. Host a private ceremony for Jackson and his family.
C. Contact the superintendent to find out if the parent's request is within the district's policy. Also, discuss the pros and cons of allowing Jackson to participate in the ceremony. Seek their advice and support.
D. Tell Jackson's mother that because he was not directly involved in the situation, he will be allowed to participate in the ceremony.
E. Other option: _____

Rigor or Relationships?

A. Trey is a friend, and his son is a great student. Make the call to the school counselor and let her know Thomas should be considered as valedictorian regardless of policy.
B. Take the policy to the school board at the next meeting and request a change to the ACT requirement for valedictorian.
C. Stick to the policy.
D. Make the executive decision and call all high school principals and let them know that you have decided to remove the ACT scores as a requirement for valedictorian and you want to make sure that all schools are aware of the change.
E. Other option: _____

Chapter 3

Lessons on Competence

Professional competence requires constant renewal for PreK–12 education leaders, whether at the elementary, middle school, or high school level. Some rise through the ranks in PreK–12 education while a few, where allowed in some states, join the ranks of PreK–12 education leaders from areas outside PreK–12 education.

Regardless of the path to leadership, these individuals must master their trade and doing so requires constant renewal and an unwavering devotion to lifelong learning. The credo of PreK–12 education leaders, like that of leaders in all areas, should be that they will remain current and thoroughly knowledgeable in their field. That they will be competent in their chosen field.

The scenarios in this chapter are, in one way or another, related to a leader's competence. If your Leader Acumen Assessment scores indicated this as an area for needed growth, you should work through the scenarios with a couple of things in mind. First, as you work through the scenarios in the chapter, take particular note of the "Contributing Authors' Options" to each problem at the end of each chapter of situational judgment tests. In working through the scenarios and reviewing the "Contributing Authors' Options," one of two things will happen. You will find disparity between your responses and the authors, or you might, indeed, find that your responses coincide with the authors' (see appendix B for a graphic representation). Next, reflect on the information you gained from the Leader Acumen Assessment. If you acknowledge that competence is an area for growth based on the assessment, ask yourself if this was based on your self-assessment, the CIRCLE assessment, or both.

If either or both assessments (the self or CIRCLE) indicate that you have room for improvement in the area of leader competence *and* you are also finding disparity in yours and the "Contributing Authors' Options," chances are you will find growth via working through these exercises and accompanying readings. However, be reminded, this will not happen overnight.

Growing your leader acumen is a worthy endeavor but is a painstakingly time-consuming undertaking. It requires rewiring of your thought processes regarding learnings that are very ingrained into your most innate understandings, and this takes time. (See appendix B for a graphic representation.)

On the other hand, if you find your solutions and the solutions offered in the "Contributing Authors' Options" coincide highly, yet your self score is lower than the mean shown at the end of your Leader Acumen Assessment for competence, one of two things is happening. Either you are lacking in self-confidence, yet your decision making is solid, or conversely, perhaps you are somewhat overconfident, but nonetheless making good decisions.

If the first is the case, working through the scenarios should enhance your self-confidence. The second option (overconfidence) is the one to be most wary of. Leaders in this category often find themselves derailed as leaders, even though they generally are good decision makers. Working through the scenarios should help to instill the idea that there is more than one acceptable solution to most problems/issues and thus lessen one potential major consequence of overconfidence, feeling that you have the only viable solution.

If you opt to have a CIRCLE/360-assessment done and find that your solutions and the solutions offered in the "Contributing Authors' Options" coincide highly, yet your CIRCLE scores were outside the standard deviation (available from the Leader Acumen Team when a CIRCLE/360-assessment is done) for competence, it is possible that a different set of problems is occurring. Either you are selecting the course of action you believe is best for the scenario, yet you would not implement it, *or* the problem may be one of perception. It is much more likely that it is the former. Only in rare instances would the latter be the case. However, we insert it here for thought because, on occasion, it is the case. And, as the old saying goes: perception is reality.

Perhaps you are indeed highly competent, yet perception is the issue for your low scores in competence. This could be a case of projection. For example, you may not "look" credible and perhaps for legitimate reasons. You will recall from the chapter on credibility in *The Soft Skills of Leadership: Navigating with Confidence and Humility*[1] that mention was made of how "what you wear" infers or projects an image. Such could be the case in this instance.

Finally, improving your leader acumen and "adaptive capacity," as stated in the preface, is a process. As you will recall, the notion of leader acumen is predicated on the theory that there is a genetic predisposition toward leadership.

As Marquis and Tilcsik[2] so aptly noted, imprinting may take place during brief sensitive periods of high susceptibility during the formative process, during the teachable moment, or another yet different time of susceptibility, and that imprints once established are persistent.

The lessons in this book are to be utilized to grow leader acumen in this third way—over the long, repetitive process. To that end and to truly be imprinted with any of the competencies, actions for building the various skillsets may be found in appendix C.

Again, quoting Maulding Green and Leonard, "true competence in effectively applying 'hard skills' requires mastery of 'soft skills'—that is, people-centered skills."[3]

COMPETENCE SITUATIONAL JUDGMENT TESTS

Inclusive Technology or a Technology No-No?

The pandemic has produced many changes in American K–12 education. However, many of those changes took place even before the pandemic. One such change was the movement away from bringing your own device practices, where school districts began providing computers (typically laptops) to all students. This practice of affording device access to all students was commonly labeled as technology inclusivity.

This practice levels the playing field to a great extent, even though some areas' lack of internet connectivity still limits what can be done on computers. The practice also led to some expected and some unexpected issues.

One such issue unexpected issue arose when a high school special education student was found to be consistently avoiding/circumventing the installed filters/blockers and viewing inappropriate material (not pornography but still inappropriate) on a school-issued computer.

As principal, what do you do?

_____
_____
_____
_____

SUGGESTED READING: Maulding Green, W., and Leonard, E. *The Soft Skills of Leadership: Navigating with Confidence and Humility*, second edition. Lanham, MD: Rowman & Littlefield, 2019, chapter 4.

ADDITIONAL SELECTED READINGS: Dimitrova, N., and Van Hooft, E. "In the Eye of the Beholder: Leader Error Orientation, Employee Perception of Leader, and Employee Work-related Outcomes." *Academy of Management Discoveries* 7, no. 4 (2021): 530–53.

Student Parking

After school hours, the school resource officer discovers a partially clothed female student sitting in a parked vehicle in the school parking lot. The other student was in the vehicle with a male, who was not a student at the school. The resource officer contacts you at home that same evening to report the incident to you as principal.

What do you do?

_____

_____

_____

_____

SUGGESTED READING: Maulding Green, W., and Leonard, E. *The Soft Skills of Leadership: Navigating with Confidence and Humility*, second edition. Lanham, MD: Rowman & Littlefield, 2019, chapter 4.

ADDITIONAL SELECTED READINGS: Rabab, A., Zahraa, A., and Mejbel, I. "The Competence of the Leader and Its Impact on the Strategic Planning of Educational Institutions." *World Bulletin of Management and Law* 13 (August 2022): 161–68.

Bullying Parent

Most school personnel understand the complexities of managing various personalities when it comes to dealing with parents. Every school has its share of parents who are difficult and who make untrue accusations against students, teachers, and administrators. Sometimes it's difficult to know when to ignore an annoying parent or when it's time to address the problem.

One of the parents of a sixth-grade student constantly complains about you. She has called the district office on multiple occasions and spreads untruths about you. For example, she told your supervisor that you are mean to her. The fact of the matter is that this parent is a bully, and she and her daughter seem incapable of telling the truth. Her daughter complains that others bully her when she gives as much as she gets.

The student refuses to follow classroom rules and procedures and has been caught several times texting her mother even though her phone is supposed to be in her backpack. You have tried different tactics over the last several months to manage the situation but have been unsuccessful, and this mother is becoming increasingly difficult.

What do you do?

_____
_____
_____
_____

SUGGESTED READING: Maulding Green, W., and Leonard, E. *The Soft Skills of Leadership: Navigating with Confidence and Humility*, second edition. Lanham, MD: Rowman & Littlefield, 2019, chapter 4.

ADDITIONAL SELECTED READINGS: Lanaj, K., Jennings, R., Ashford, S., and Krishnan, S. "When Leader Self-care Begets Other Care: Leader Role Self-compassion and Helping at Work." *Journal of Applied Psychology* 107, no. 9 (2022): 1543–60.

Cleanliness Is a Virtue

The cleanliness of a school is very important to the school's image. When people walk into the building, they immediately notice how the school looks.

Your most recently hired custodian is a huge disappointment. She was hired last summer but gets very little work done on any given day. The teachers in her hallway report that she only takes out their trash but doesn't clean their classrooms. She has three well-known hiding places, and you, in fact, have caught her in one of these hiding places.

In addition to not getting work done, her attitude toward you is very disrespectful. Even after discussion with her regarding her behavior, her tone of voice commonly is insulting. You are tired of it. You asked your assistant principal (her direct supervisor) to talk to her about her work on two previous occasions; although he did, the problem has not improved.

You have reminded her that she is a probationary employee and have given her ample warnings, both verbal and written, that there is a strong possibility she may be terminated. However, it is unlikely that you will be able to replace her until next summer because good custodians are few and far between. Additionally, one of your other custodians is on extended leave, so losing this custodian would leave you two custodians short for the remainder of the school year in a very large building.

What do you do?

_____
_____
_____
_____

SUGGESTED READING: Maulding Green, W., and Leonard, E. *The Soft Skills of Leadership: Navigating with Confidence and Humility*, second edition. Lanham, MD: Rowman & Littlefield, 2019, chapter 4.

ADDITIONAL SELECTED READINGS: Ong, C., Roberts, R., Woodman, T., and Arthur, C. "The Leader Ship Was Destined to Sink: An Examination of Dominance and Prestige on the Rise and Fall of the Narcissistic Leader." *Group Dynamics: Theory, Research, and Practice* (December 2021).

A Place to Start

Often, school administrators find themselves in the position of weighing the best interest of one student against the best interest of all students. Resources available can also make it difficult to serve special education students in their actual least restrictive environment.

Brandon, a sixth grader, enrolled at Pineville Elementary at the beginning of this school year. He had been in several schools out of state and had an individual education plan (IEP), which documented behavioral issues. His mother told administrators that in his previous school he had been in a self-contained classroom "for his behavior."

While waiting for his IEP to arrive from the previous school, Brandon was placed in the regular classroom per the recommendation of the special education director of the district. During the few days in the regular classroom, it was found that Brandon had significant deficits in reading as well as behavioral issues that required almost one-on-one attention. Pineville Elementary has only one self-contained classroom, which serves only students with severe cognitive deficits which Brandon does not have.

What do you do?

_____
_____
_____
_____

SUGGESTED READING: Maulding Green, W., and Leonard, E. *The Soft Skills of Leadership: Navigating with Confidence and Humility*, second edition. Lanham, MD: Rowman & Littlefield, 2019, chapter 4.

ADDITIONAL SELECTED READINGS: Eichenauer, C., Ryan, A., and Alanis, J. "Leadership During Crisis: An Examination of Supervisory Leadership Behavior and Gender During COVID-19." *Journal of Leadership & Organizational Studies* 29, no. 2 (2022): 190–207.

Hot Head

You have a meeting with a teacher in your school because it has been reported by another teacher that the teacher you are meeting with has been having outbursts in front of the students. In your meeting with this teacher, you learn about outside family stressors and physical ailments that have been exhausting him mentally. He also mentions that this group of students is different from last year while sharing that "they don't listen" and require constant redirection.

You remind him of his worth in the building and that the students love his class. You gently remind him to use his sick days to take care of himself and that lead teachers are available to offer classroom management strategies and objective observations. He says things are about to improve for him at home and that he should be fine. The conversation is noted, and the superintendent is made aware.

A few weeks pass and the same reporting teacher shares more outbursts by the teacher you conferenced with earlier. This time, however, the reporter shares that there is profanity and slamming doors. You ask the reporting teacher to write her statement and inquire if there were any other witnesses. At this point, you let your superintendent know that there may be a situation where a teacher suspension may be warranted.

The superintendent meets with you and the teacher. The teacher acknowledges that he has been losing his cool more frequently but denies using profanity. A formal letter is placed in the file stating another occurrence will result in termination. In the meantime, he is temporarily suspended with pay.

A few weeks pass and all is well. You check on him often, offering an encouraging word. You feel like things are improving.

Four days before a scheduled break, a teacher (different than the previous one) reports outbursts with profanity. The teacher reports this incident at end of day. You recognize this allegation will result in termination.

What should you do?

_____
_____
_____
_____

SUGGESTED READING: Maulding Green, W., and Leonard, E. *The Soft Skills of Leadership: Navigating with Confidence and Humility*, second edition. Lanham, MD: Rowman & Littlefield, 2019, chapter 4.

ADDITIONAL SELECTED READINGS: Hetrick, A. L., Blocker, L. D., Fairchild, J., and Hunter, S. T. "To Apologize or Justify: Leader Responses to Task and Relational Mistakes." *Basic & Applied Social Psychology* 43, no. 1 (2021): 30–45.

Christmas Party

It's the last day of school before Christmas vacation. The teachers and children are ready for their party. Parents are pulling into the parking lot to bring in cupcakes and other party foods and games. At the same time, you have been notified by local police that there was a man spotted on a rural road with a shotgun a few miles from the school. However, it is hunting season and the school is a rural school.

What do you do?

_____
_____
_____
_____

SUGGESTED READING: Maulding Green, W., and Leonard, E. *The Soft Skills of Leadership: Navigating with Confidence and Humility*, second edition. Lanham, MD: Rowman & Littlefield, 2019, chapter 4.

ADDITIONAL SELECTED READINGS: Chen, H., Qiaozhuan, L., Feng, C., and Zhang, Y. "Why and When Do Employees Become More Proactive Under Humble Leaders? The Roles of Psychological Need Satisfaction and Chinese Traditionality." *Journal of Organizational Change Management* 34, no. 5 (2021): 1076–95.

CONTRIBUTING AUTHORS' OPTIONS FOR COMPETENCE SITUATIONAL JUDGMENT TESTS

Inclusive Technology or a Technology No-No?

A. Discipline the student as called for by the disciplinary code, including taking up the computer permanently.
B. As an interim step, take away the computer. Call an IEP meeting, and if appropriate, discipline the student as called for by the disciplinary code. Return the computer to the student but only to be used when under the direct supervision of a teacher at school or a parent at home.

C. As an interim step, take away the computer. Call an IEP meeting, and if appropriate, discipline the student as called for by the disciplinary code. Return the computer to the student but only to be used when under the direct supervision of a teacher at school.
D. As an interim step, take away the computer and install stronger filters/blockers. Call an IEP meeting, and if appropriate, discipline the student as called for by the disciplinary code and return the computer to the student.
E. Refer the student to a counselor who can determine why the student is seeking this material. Based on the counselor's recommendations, act accordingly.

Student Parking

A. Notify the parent(s) of the incident and warn them that if any future incidents occur, the student will be suspended from school.
B. Verbally reprimand the student but take no further action.
C. Interview the student, then based on the report of the resource officer, suspend the student per term afforded by district policy.
D. Interview the student, then based on the report of the resource officer, send the student to the systems' alternative school per term afforded by district policy.
E. Interview the student, then based on the report of the resource officer, send the student to in-school suspension per term afforded by district policy.
F. Notify the police of the incident.

Bullying Parent

A. Because this problem has gone on for a few months, and you have been unable to remedy the situation, you decide to talk to your supervisor to see what she suggests.
B. Call the mother and schedule a meeting with her to discuss what she has been saying about you.
C. Just ignore the problem. Parents will say what they say, and there is nothing you can do about it.
D. Give this woman a taste of her own medicine. Tell her exactly what you think of her and her daughter.

Cleanliness Is a Virtue

A. Call human resources and have them terminate her.
B. Talk to her again and give her another chance but now begin documenting.
C. Begin cleaning the classrooms yourself.
D. Have the other custodians pick up her slack.

A Place to Start

A. Leave Brandon in the regular class permanently and hope he catches up.
B. Involve the behavior specialist to get input for behavior goals and interventions.
C. Consider a placement at the district alternative school for a transitional period.
D. Place Brandon in a lower grade so that he can get the academic interventions that he needs.

Hot Head

A. Contact the teacher that evening and ask him to stay home through break.
B. You hate to fire him, so you remove him from classroom responsibilities and assign him another role in the building.
C. Contact the teacher that evening, ask him to stay home, and conduct a thorough investigation to include statements from witnesses and contact the superintendent.

Christmas Party

A. Immediately put the school on lockdown, turn off all lights, put kids in their safe spot, keep parents in their vehicles, and wait for more information from the police.
B. Usher all parents from the parking lot into the school, allow Christmas parties to take place in the rooms, keep the school doors locked, and remain vigilant and in close contact with the police. At the same time, make an announcement for teachers to check their emails and send an email to teachers to notify them of the situation and instruct them to close their blinds and keep their doors locked.
C. It is hunting season and in a rural area. Let the festivities go on.

Chapter 4

Lessons on Ability to Inspire

When our intent as a leader is to inspire, we often fall short of our goal. For some reason, as leaders, we believe that inspiration is some mystical/magical force that only coaches and motivational speakers possess. Although inspiration can sometimes include the elements of high energy and mountain-moving motivation, inspiration is best achieved through what we do and say.

The scenarios in this chapter are in one way or another, related to a leader's ability to inspire. If your Leader Acumen Assessment scores indicated this as an area for needed growth, you should work through the scenarios with a couple of things in mind. First, as you work through the scenarios in the chapter take particular note of the "Contributing Authors' Options" to each problem at the end of each chapter of situational judgment tests.

In working through the scenarios and reviewing the "Contributing Authors' Options," one of two things will happen. You will find disparity between your responses and the authors, or you might, indeed, find that your responses coincide with the authors' (see appendix B for a graphic representation). Next, reflect on the information you gained from the Leader Acumen Assessment. If you acknowledge that ability to inspire is an area for growth based on the assessment, ask yourself if this was based on your self-assessment, the CIRCLE assessment, or both.

If either or both assessments (the self or CIRCLE) indicate that you have room for improvement in the area of leader ability to inspire *and* you are also finding disparity in yours and the "Contributing Authors' Options," chances are you will find growth via working through these exercises and accompanying readings.

However, be reminded, this will not happen overnight. Growing your leader acumen is a worthy endeavor but is a painstakingly time-consuming undertaking. It requires rewiring of your thought processes regarding learnings that are very ingrained into your most innate understandings, and this takes time. (See appendix B for a graphic representation.)

On the other hand, if you find your solutions and the solutions offered in the "Contributing Authors' Options" coincide highly, yet your self score is lower than the mean shown at the end of your Leader Acumen Assessment for ability to inspire, one of two things is happening. Either you are lacking in self-confidence, yet your decision making is solid, or conversely, perhaps you are somewhat overconfident, but nonetheless making good decisions.

If the first is the case, working through the scenarios should enhance your self-confidence. The second option (overconfidence) is the one to be most wary of. Leaders in this category often find themselves derailed as leaders, even though they generally are good decision makers. Working through the scenarios should help to instill the idea that there is more than one acceptable solution to most problems/issues and thus lessen one potential major consequence of overconfidence, feeling that you have the only viable solution.

If you opt to have a CIRCLE/360-assessment done and find that your solutions and the solutions offered in the "Contributing Authors' Options" coincide highly, yet your CIRCLE scores were outside the standard deviation (available from the Leader Acumen Team when a CIRCLE/360-assessment is done) for ability to inspire, it is possible that a different set of problems is occurring. Either you are selecting the course of action you believe is best for the scenario, yet in reality you would not implement it, *or* the problem may be one of perception. It is much more likely that it is the former. Only in rare instances would the latter be the case. However, we insert it here for thought because, on occasion, it is the case. And, as the old saying goes: perception is reality.

Perhaps you are indeed highly inspirational, yet perception is the issue for your low scores in ability to inspire. This could be a case of projection. For example, you may not "look" inspirational and perhaps for legitimate reasons. You will recall from the chapter on credibility in *The Soft Skills of Leadership: Navigating with Confidence and Humility*, second edition,[1] that mention was made of how "what you wear" infers or projects an image. Such could be the case in this instance.

Finally, improving your leader acumen and "adaptive capacity," as stated in the preface, is a process. As you will recall, the notion of leader acumen is predicated on the theory that there is a genetic predisposition toward leadership.

As Marquis and Tilcsik[2] so aptly noted, imprinting may take place during brief sensitive periods of high susceptibility during the formative process, during the teachable moment, or another yet different time of susceptibility, and that imprints once established are persistent. The lessons in this book are to be utilized to grow leader acumen in this third way—over the long, repetitive process. To that end and to truly be imprinted with any of the competencies, actions for building the various skillsets may be found in appendix C.

"True inspiration for both the leader and peers and followers comes from within by finding value and meaning in the work they do."[3]

ABILITY TO INSPIRE SITUATIONAL JUDGMENT TESTS

Guilt by Association?

Darren is a junior and comes in to tell you (as principal) that Joe, a senior, has a gun in his backpack. You ask Darren how he knew about the gun, and he said that he saw it and described it as a stainless steel semi-automatic pistol. Joe apparently opened his bookbag in algebra class and showed the gun in the bottom of the bag. You ask when this took place and Darren says yesterday. Darren said that Manny also saw the gun.

You ask Darren to write a report and immediately ask the school resource officer to go get Joe out of class. You also bring Manny in and ask him if he saw the gun. He affirms he saw it in the bottom of Joe's bookbag. You ask him to write a report as well. You search Joe and he does not have the gun. Through questioning, Joe admits that he did have a gun the day before but left it at home today. He is arrested and the police find the gun at his house.

You notice that Manny's written report says that Darren showed him Joe's gun. In questioning Manny how Darren showed it to him he says that Darren unzipped Joe's bookbag and pulled the gun out and showed him as they were walking down the hall. Joe was walking and Darren just reached in unprovoked to show the gun. Manny felt like Darren was showing off.

Joe was suspended indefinitely and put up for expulsion the following day. What do you do with Darren? If it wasn't for him, you wouldn't know about the gun. However, you have a witness that directly states that Darren is handling the gun. You were able to find the scene on security cameras and see Darren go in the book bag to show Manny, but you were not able to see the gun because of the angle.

What do you do?

_____
_____
_____
_____

SUGGESTED READING: Maulding Green, W., and Leonard, E. *The Soft Skills of Leadership: Navigating with Confidence and Humility*, second edition. Lanham, MD: Rowman & Littlefield, 2019, chapter 5.

ADDITIONAL SELECTED READINGS: Karaszewski, R., and Drewniak, R. "The Leading Traits of the Modern Corporate Leader: Comparing Survey Results from 2008 and 2018." Energies 14, no. 23 (2021): 7926.

One-to-One: A Blessing or a Curse?

During the COVID-19 pandemic, school districts worked diligently to put electronic devices in the hands of all students so educators could continue teaching and communicating with their students virtually. Having access to technology twenty-four hours a day, seven days a week provides opportunities for education to extend beyond the four walls of the classroom.

However, what other doors are being opened? Access to technology also allows students unlimited access to the internet and the ability to search subjects or participate in activities that the school district does not promote. To discourage this, many districts purchased programs that alert administrators any time of day or night if a student searches an inappropriate subject; types inappropriate words into a document, chat room, or game; or if the student types some form of "kill myself."

As an assistant principal, you have chosen to check emails on the weekend and after hours because returning to work with hundreds of emails to check is overwhelming. Other administrators do not consistently check their emails outside of work hours. While visiting out-of-state family, you receive an email from this system that a student, who is not a student assigned to you, is contemplating suicide.

What do you do?

_____
_____
_____
_____

SUGGESTED READING: Maulding Green, W., and Leonard, E. *The Soft Skills of Leadership: Navigating with Confidence and Humility*, second edition. Lanham, MD: Rowman & Littlefield, 2019, chapter 5.

ADDITIONAL SELECTED READINGS: Svajone, B., Meidute-Kavaliauskiene, I., and Hošková-Mayerová, S. "Military Leader Behavior Formation for Sustainable Country Security." Sustainability 13, no. 8 (2021): 4521.

Team Spirit

There are several ways to handle discipline issues in a school environment; however, the main purpose of any form of discipline enforced should be with the sole purpose of altering the behavior of the students so they are encouraged to make better decisions in the future. When a student has fulfilled the requirements of the punishment received, the student should be treated in a manner that is conducive for that child to be successful in school and should be afforded any and all opportunities made available to other students.

The way a student is treated after a negative behavioral incident could make the difference between whether the student is successful in continuing their education and enjoys school.

A ninth-grade student (who had struggled with behavior issues in middle school) has been encouraged to try out for several school team sports in order to provide him with needed discipline and accountability. He has proven to have natural athletic abilities, and the support of the coaches and team members has helped to keep him focused in school and out of trouble this year.

After one of the football games, this student went to the opposing team's bus while in uniform and yelled profanities at the players in response to an interaction that had happened while on the field. When confronted by school leaders, he continued his cursing. He continued even when approached by the sheriff that was working the game that night. The student's punishment required him to spend forty-five days at the alternative school. He was not allowed to play football or attend any school functions during this time.

While at the alternative school, he did his work, came to school regularly, and did not have any discipline write-ups. When his forty-five days were over at the alternative school, the student asked if he could join the basketball team.

What would you do?

_____
_____
_____
_____

SUGGESTED READING: Maulding Green, W., and Leonard, E. *The Soft Skills of Leadership: Navigating with Confidence and Humility*, second edition. Lanham, MD: Rowman & Littlefield, 2019, chapter 5.

ADDITIONAL SELECTED READINGS: Tohatan, A. "The Qualities of Contemporary Leadership. Comparative Analysis between Employee Assessments and Leaders' Self-Assessment." *Asian Journal of Economics, Finance and Management* 7, no. 2 (2022): 46–53.

The Digital Age

Online student safety is a top priority for your district. A new program is purchased which alerts administrators through email if a student types anything inappropriate, bullies, or suggests self-harm while using a district device.

Over Thanksgiving break, you receive an email alert while watching the evening news that a student is searching the "quickest way to hang yourself." You have received email alerts earlier in the school year for this same student searching topics related to depression.

What do you do?

_____
_____
_____
_____

SUGGESTED READING: Maulding Green, W., and Leonard, E. *The Soft Skills of Leadership: Navigating with Confidence and Humility*, second edition. Lanham, MD: Rowman & Littlefield, 2019, chapter 5.

ADDITIONAL SELECTED READINGS: Tongtong, Z., and Halimah, M. "Transformational and Transactional Leadership Toward the Enhancement of Followers' Trust and Psychological Well-being." *Higher Education and Oriental Studies (HEOS)* 2, no. 2 (2022): 67–74.

Proselytizing Physical Education Coach

As the school leader (principal) and someone who values health and fitness, you understand the need for students to have an engaging and effective physical education program. There are many benefits to a solid program: better behaved students who can have fun and become physically stronger and healthier while also making academic gains.

It is alleged that your basketball coach had one of his players write "The Lord's Prayer" ten times because the player got in minor trouble in one of his classes. The parent of this player called you to complain. The coach has had other issues in other schools and districts, and this is only his second year at your school.

You don't know why the coach has been so transient during his career, but you suspect it's because of his unconventional coaching methods. He has a strong rapport with his players and families, though, and you want to keep him. However, he is a veteran teacher and should know that he cannot proselytize in public school.

What do you do?

SUGGESTED READING: Maulding Green, W., and Leonard, E. *The Soft Skills of Leadership: Navigating with Confidence and Humility*, second edition. Lanham, MD: Rowman & Littlefield, 2019, chapter 5.

ADDITIONAL SELECTED READINGS: Bak, H., Jin, M., and McDonald III, B. "Unpacking the Transformational Leadership-Innovative Work Behavior Relationship: The Mediating Role of Psychological Capital." *Public Performance & Management Review* 45, no. 1 (2022): 80–105.

Donating Sick Days

Your new assistant principal is pregnant with twins. She comes to tell you (as principal) that there are complications, and she will need to be out for an extended time. You advise her to meet with human resources, and you will talk to the superintendent about your plans.

However, before you meet with the superintendent, teachers come to you in distress. The assistant principal has been reported going individually to the teachers to ask them to donate sick days to her since she will need to be out. In return she would "take care" of them in the future. The teachers say that they feel threatened if they do not donate days to her.

What do you do?

SUGGESTED READING: Maulding Green, W., and Leonard, E. *The Soft Skills of Leadership: Navigating with Confidence and Humility*, second edition. Lanham, MD: Rowman & Littlefield, 2019, chapter 5.

ADDITIONAL SELECTED READINGS: Barton, D. "Character: A Muscle Leaders Must Develop." *Organizational Dynamics* 50, no. 3 (2021): 1–7.

Close to Home

Starting a new position is hard. Starting a leadership position within your home district can be even harder. In this new position, you are required to hold accountable individuals whom you have known most of your life and a year ago were your peers. These individuals have trusted you with personal and professional information over the years, sought counsel from you, and through all of this, strong relationships have been built.

Entering into this leadership position, you know that the conversations are going to become more difficult. The level of responsibility you have has increased and so must the level of accountability for those you serve.

Serving as the new middle school principal, you have received a message from a very vocal parent that their child has been inappropriately touched by another thirteen-year-old student of the same sex on multiple occasions. Though you have just received this information, you learn that the parent has already shared on Facebook that you would do nothing about it because you were just going to cover up for your teacher friends.

Both students are in Mrs. Baker's classroom. Mrs. Baker is a childhood friend, coach to your daughter's basketball team, and for the last eight years was your co-teacher. You begin your investigation only to find out that Mrs. Baker was made aware of these incidents by the child's parents on each occasion. When interviewing Mrs. Baker about the incidents, you question why she didn't document and report these incidents to the office.

She responded by saying, "I know how busy you are, and I talked to both of the kids the last time Mom called and they were okay." You remind Mrs. Baker how serious the district takes reports of possible abuse and that she is obligated to report.

How do you proceed?

_____
_____
_____
_____

SUGGESTED READING: Maulding Green, W., and Leonard, E. *The Soft Skills of Leadership: Navigating with Confidence and Humility*, second edition. Lanham, MD: Rowman & Littlefield, 2019, chapter 5.

ADDITIONAL SELECTED READINGS: Thiel, C., Prince, N., and Sahatjian, Z. "The (Electronic) Walls between Us: How Employee Monitoring Undermines Ethical Leadership." *Human Resource Management Journal* 1 (2022).

Grieving

Leadership comes with twists and turns we just can't anticipate despite our best efforts to be proactive and plan. When school or district leaders make decisions, they must consider all stakeholders as well as the politics of the district while considering the question, "What is best for students?" No matter what decision must be made, from athletics to policy, buses to buildings, what is best for students should shape our decisions.

As superintendent, you made the decision to remove a building principal from her position at the end of the first semester. This decision did not come easy, and the process was painful for both you and for her. She was loved within her community, but the school was headed in the wrong direction and despite your efforts to help her, she was not willing to change.

In January, only four weeks after the principal had been removed, a veteran teacher of twenty-six years unexpectedly passed away on a Sunday afternoon. This teacher was the heart and soul of this same elementary school, and the news devastated the staff and the community. Immediately after hearing the news, you receive messages from staff members wanting to know how they are to share this information with students the next day.

The teachers were devastated, and they didn't have a building leader to lean on. Many of them asked if they could take off the next day because they didn't want to have to face each student and tell the story over and over.

As a district leader, how do you meet the needs of students and staff during this tragedy?

_____
_____
_____
_____

SUGGESTED READING: Maulding Green, W., and Leonard, E. *The Soft Skills of Leadership: Navigating with Confidence and Humility*, second edition. Lanham, MD: Rowman & Littlefield, 2019, chapter 5.

ADDITIONAL SELECTED READINGS: Polman, P., and Winston, A. "Becoming a Courageous, Net Positive Leader." *Leader to Leader* 103 (2022): 25–30.

Never Give Up

As administrators, we never want to give up on a student. However, when a student is troubled, there is a fine line between doing what is best for the student and the hope that something will change where the student starts taking their education seriously. The choices of the leader in these situations go a long way in determining how that leader is viewed by those in the community. Is the leader really concerned about what is best for the student, or does the leader simply have what is best for the school in mind?

Jose Hernandez is a junior in high school. It is February, and counselors are already looking at scheduling for the following school year. You are the director of career and technical education (CTE) for the district, and Jose is in year two of the welding program. He has already been accepted into the year three program, which is sponsored by a local defense contractor. This organization sponsors a program for senior CTE students culminating in a job offer above other entry-level hires.

Jose will be twenty years old at the start of the next school year because he was held back in elementary and failed his seventh-grade year. As director of CTE, you are brought in on a conference call with Jose, his parents, the high school principal, counselor, and English language learner coordinator. Jose is currently failing all his classes and, to graduate, must pass all these as well as the classes on his schedule for his senior year. It is suggested that Jose drop out, start prepping for a GED, and go to work.

Knowing Jose since middle school, you are aware that no one in his family has graduated from high school. He really wants to graduate and get offered the position because the pay and benefits will be life changing for Jose and his family. You are also aware that he is a very talented welder, and the organization is enthusiastic about a potential offer as well. If he does not stay in school, go through the program, and graduate, he will not have this opportunity.

What do you do?

_____
_____
_____

SUGGESTED READING: Maulding Green, W., and Leonard, E. *The Soft Skills of Leadership: Navigating with Confidence and Humility*, second edition. Lanham, MD: Rowman & Littlefield, 2019, chapter 5.

ADDITIONAL SELECTED READINGS: Bakker, A., Hetland, J., Olsen, O., and Espevik, R. "Daily Transformational Leadership: A Source of Inspiration for Follower Performance?" *European Management Journal* (2022).

CONTRIBUTING AUTHORS' OPTIONS FOR ABILITY TO INSPIRE SITUATIONAL JUDGMENT TESTS

Guilt by Association?

A. Suspend Darren indefinitely and recommend expulsion.

B. Place Darren in in-school suspension for twenty days.
C. Suspend Darren for ten days.
D. Place Darren in alternative school for forty-five days.
E. Do nothing at all.

One-to-One: A Blessing or a Curse?

A. Do not act because that makes you liable for all alerts and puts you at risk of being sued.
B. Do not act because you deserve vacation time with your family, and he is not one of the students assigned to you.
C. Text your administrative team, which includes your principal.
D. Call the parent immediately.
E. Call the police immediately.

Team Spirit

A. Deny the request due to the nature of the offense that happened while he was on the football team.
B. Allow the student to join the basketball team when he returns to regular school.
C. Allow the student to join the basketball team but don't let him play in any games due to his behavior at the football game.
D. Make an example out of the student by not allowing him on any sports team due to his inappropriate behavior and hope that others will learn from his mistake.
E. Don't allow the student to join the team this year but allow him to try out for the team for next year if he doesn't have any behavior issues for the remainder of the year.

The Digital Age

A. You do nothing because this happens during Thanksgiving break.
B. You address the issue when you return to school from break.
C. You contact the student's parents immediately.
D. You email the student and let them know you are concerned for their welfare.

Proselytizing Physical Education Coach

A. Don't say anything to the coach and ignore the problem. Surely the coach won't do it again.

B. Call the supervisor of the physical education department and ask her to handle the situation.
C. Tell the parent that you will talk to the coach and handle the situation, but then don't say anything to the coach.
D. Have the coach come to your office and talk through the problem. Perhaps it's best to hear his side of the story before making a final decision.

Donating Sick Days

A. Explain to teachers that they are not obligated to donate days, and just let it go since the assistant principal is in a risky health situation.
B. Explain to teachers that they are not obligated to donate days, and talk to the superintendent about the situation.
C. Explain to teachers that they are not obligated to donate days, and have a conversation with the assistant principal and advise her to stop asking for days from the teachers.

Close to Home

A. Report to the parents that it was no big deal, and that Mrs. Baker said she would handle it in her classroom.
B. Now that you are aware that the incidents did indeed happen, you should place a call to Child Protective Services and put the teacher on administrative leave until the investigation is complete.
C. Encourage the teacher to bring the students into her room and talk about appropriate/inappropriate touching.
D. Invite the parents of both students to your office so that you can explain to both of them how great Mrs. Baker is as a teacher, and that if there was anything to the allegations, she would have reported it.

Grieving

A. Appoint a district office employee to go out and address the staff at the beginning of the day.
B. Allow staff to take off that day and hire substitutes to fill the classes.
C. As the district leader, you address the staff and student needs face-to-face the next morning.
D. Ask a local pastor in the community to address teachers and students.

Never Give Up

A. As director of CTE, he is technically not your student so whatever the high school feels is best is fine.
B. Ask the high school to give him a chance to pull the grades up and hold the decision with regard to dropping out until the end of the year.
C. As director of CTE, when Jose is in your facility, have your student services coordinators offer him tutoring so he can get his grades up continue in school.
D. As director of CTE, get with one of your business/industry partners and see if there are jobs available somewhere for Jose.
E. Ask the high school to give him a chance to pull the grades up and hold the decision about dropping out until the end of the year. And as director of CTE, when Jose is in your facility, have your student services coordinators offer him tutoring so he can get his grades up to continue in school.

Chapter 5

Lessons on Vision

In *The Soft Skills of Leadership: Navigating with Confidence and Humility*, second edition, the authors share that "Vision as defined in the LA model is the end result of a process whereby a leader develops objectives or goals and sets a direction for an organization based on the shared input of all stakeholders. Defining vision is simple. Creating a shared vision and, more significantly, effectively communicating that shared vision, and transforming it into action is the challenge."[1]

The scenarios in this chapter are, in one way or another, related to a leader's vision. If your Leader Acumen Assessment scores indicated this as an area for needed growth, you should work through the scenarios with a couple of things in mind. First, as you work through the scenarios in the chapter, take particular note of the "Contributing Authors' Options" to each problem at the end of each chapter of situational judgment tests.

In working through the scenarios and reviewing the "Contributing Authors' Options," one of two things will happen. You will find disparity between your responses and the authors, or you might, indeed, find that your responses coincide with the authors' (see appendix B for a graphic representation). Next, reflect on the information you gained from the Leader Acumen Assessment. If you acknowledge that vision is an area for growth based on the assessment, ask yourself if this was based on your self-assessment, the CIRCLE assessment, or both.

If either or both assessments (the self or CIRCLE) indicate that you have room for improvement in the area of leader vision *and* you are also finding disparity in yours and the "Contributing Authors' Options," chances are you will find growth via working through these exercises and accompanying readings.

However, be reminded that this will not happen overnight. Growing your leader acumen is a worthy endeavor but is a painstakingly time-consuming undertaking. It requires rewiring of your thought processes regarding learnings that are very ingrained into your most innate understandings and this takes time. (See appendix B for a graphic representation.)

On the other hand, if you find your solutions and the solutions offered in the "Contributing Authors' Options" coincide highly, yet your self score is lower than the mean shown at the end of your Leader Acumen Assessment for vision, one of two things is happening. Either you are lacking in self-confidence, yet your decision making is solid, or conversely, perhaps you are somewhat overconfident, but nonetheless making good decisions.

If the first is the case, working through the scenarios should enhance your self-confidence. The second option (overconfidence) is the one to be most wary of. Leaders in this category many times find themselves derailed as leaders, even though they generally are good decision makers. Working through the scenarios should help to instill the idea that there is more than one acceptable solution to most problems/issues and thus lessen one potential major consequence of overconfidence, feeling that you have the only viable solution.

If you opt to have a CIRCLE/360-assessment done and find that your solutions and the solutions offered in the "Contributing Authors' Options" coincide highly, yet your CIRCLE scores were outside the standard deviation (available from the Leader Acumen Team when a Circle/360-assessment is done) for vision, it is possible that a different set of problems is occurring. Either you are selecting the course of action you believe is best for the scenario, yet in reality you would not implement it, *or* the problem may be one of perception. It is much more likely that it is the former. Only in rare instances would the latter be the case. However, we insert it here for thought because, on occasion, it is the case. And, as the old saying goes: perception is reality.

Perhaps you are indeed highly visionary yet perception is the issue for your low scores in vision. This could be a case of projection. For example, you may not "look" visionary and perhaps for legitimate reasons. You will recall from the chapter on credibility in *The Soft Skills of Leadership: Navigating with Confidence and Humility*, second edition,[2] that mention was made of how "what you wear" infers or projects an image. Such could be the case in this instance.

Finally, improving your leader acumen and "adaptive capacity" as stated in the preface is a process. As you will recall, the notion of leader acumen is predicated on the theory that there is a genetic predisposition toward leadership.

As Marquis and Tilcsik[3] so aptly noted, imprinting may take place during brief sensitive periods of high susceptibility during the formative process, during the teachable moment, or another yet different time of susceptibility, and that imprints once established are persistent.

The lessons in this book are to be utilized to grow leader acumen in this third way—over the long, repetitive process. To that end and to truly be imprinted with any of the competencies, actions for building the various skillsets may be found in appendix C.

"Vision opens the door to opportunities for success for the credible, competent, inspirational leader."[4]

VISION SITUATIONAL JUDGMENT TESTS

Late Night Call

Calls after midnight are always alarming for a school leader. The phone rings, and it is one of your school's teachers who says she has received a distressing Facebook message stating no one should go to school tomorrow because there will be a shooting. The teacher is panicking and asking what she should do. She is concerned that it may be true, and she is concerned for her students, as well as her own children who attend the school.

What do you do?

_____
_____
_____
_____

SUGGESTED READING: Maulding Green, W., and Leonard, E. *The Soft Skills of Leadership: Navigating with Confidence and Humility*, second edition. Lanham, MD: Rowman & Littlefield, 2019, chapter 6.

ADDITIONAL SELECTED READINGS: Guo, L., Mao, J., Huang, Q., and Zhang, G. "Polishing Followers' Future Work Selves! The Critical Roles of Leader Future Orientation and Vision Communication." *Journal of Vocational Behavior* 137 (September 2022): 1–12.

Digital Tracking

One of the responsibilities of a superintendent is to ensure enforcement of the rights of employees. This must be done while concurrently guaranteeing the safety and security of the children of the district. Occasionally, these responsibilities come into conflict with one another.

The local law enforcement agent calls you (the superintendent) with a report that a teacher within the district has been tracked digitally as having child pornography in his possession. The officer states that the teacher will be arrested today. The agent in charge has agreed to wait until the teacher leaves school; the arrest will be made at home.

Note: This employee's parent is a long-time administrator in the district and a friend. Along with the obvious issues at hand, there will be media attention to which you will be required to respond.

What do you do?

_____
_____
_____
_____

SUGGESTED READING: Maulding Green, W., and Leonard, E. *The Soft Skills of Leadership: Navigating with Confidence and Humility*, second edition. Lanham, MD: Rowman & Littlefield, 2019, chapter 6.

ADDITIONAL SELECTED READINGS: Lo, L. "What Makes a Leader? An Exploratory Study of Academic Library Employees' Perceptions." *Portal: Libraries & the Academy* 22, no. 2 (2022): 375–94.

FaceTime

A student is assigned to the system's alternative school for threatening a teacher. While at the alternative school, the student has chronic absenteeism, is passive-aggressive toward staff, and will not do his work. Moreover, when in attendance, the student goes on basketball websites multiple times daily.

Each time, he is removed from the sites and redirected to his assigned work. The high school basketball coach is brought in on more than one occasion for intervention with the student. The parents have been contacted multiple times. The student maintains failing grades and defiance toward the staff. One day, the student logs onto FaceTime to talk with someone. Staff immediately closes out the student's account and reprimands the student. As soon as staff walks away from the student, the student goes right back onto FaceTime.

What do you do?

_____
_____
_____
_____

SUGGESTED READING: Maulding Green, W., and Leonard, E. *The Soft Skills of Leadership: Navigating with Confidence and Humility*, second edition. Lanham, MD: Rowman & Littlefield, 2019, chapter 6.

ADDITIONAL SELECTED READINGS: Eddy, P., VanDerLinden, K., and Hartman, C. "Changing Definitions of Leadership or Same Old 'Hero' Leader?" *Community College Review* 1 (2022).

Missing in Action

Mrs. Dallas is a teacher you have been closely monitoring as a probationary teacher. You have already put Mrs. Dallas on a coaching cycle for grading issues. Mrs. Dallas is a talented teacher; however, she does not believe in late work. She does not accept any work that is not turned in on time, and students do not get any type of partial credit or reduced points. The classes she teaches are not advanced or pre-AP.

Several students have Individual Education Plans or receive 504 accommodations. After completing her coaching cycle reinforcing the importance of accepting late work for partial credit or a reduced grade, she reverts back to "all or nothing." As principal, you have decided to non-renew Mrs. Dallas.

The school district you work for believes in informing non-renewed teachers the last week in April, giving them time to find a new job. Upon informing Mrs. Dallas she was to be non-renewed, she comes to work the following day but then does not return at all. There are twenty-five days left in semester. Over 50 percent of the students are failing in all three of her classes.

What do you do?

_____
_____
_____
_____

SUGGESTED READING: Maulding Green, W., and Leonard, E. *The Soft Skills of Leadership: Navigating with Confidence and Humility*, second edition. Lanham, MD: Rowman & Littlefield, 2019, chapter 6.

ADDITIONAL SELECTED READINGS: Caviglia-Harris, J., Hodges, E., Helmuth, B., Bennett, E., Galvin, K., Krebs, M., Lips, K., Lowman, M., Schulte, L., and Schuur, E. "The Six Dimensions of Collective Leadership that Advance Sustainability Objectives: Rethinking What It Means to be an Academic Leader." *Ecology & Society* 26, no. 3 (2021): 99–112.

Savvy School Counselor

Much of the success of a school depends on a comprehensive school counseling program. As the school principal, you deeply value a strong school counselor who truly understands the needs of the students in your building. Your goal is to have a school counselor who is committed to student learning and is willing to go the extra mile to help all students experience success in school.

However, you have noticed that your school counselor is coasting. Most of the time she just walks around campus and visits faculty, staff, and students. Her counseling program is not strong, and you are frustrated with her lack of initiative in maintaining a high-quality school counseling program. She is highly intelligent and capable of being an effective school counselor. However, she is a veteran counselor and is nearing retirement, so you need to carefully manage the situation because there are very few good school counselors you could hire to replace her.

What do you do?

_____
_____
_____
_____

SUGGESTED READING: Maulding Green, W., and Leonard, E. *The Soft Skills of Leadership: Navigating with Confidence and Humility*, second edition. Lanham, MD: Rowman & Littlefield, 2019, chapter 6.

ADDITIONAL SELECTED READING: Kim, J., Waldman, D., Balthazard, P., and Ames J. "Leader Self-projection and Collective Role Performance: A Consideration of Visionary Leadership." *The Leadership Quarterly* (2022).

Does All Really Mean All?

The River City School District is one of four districts in the state that have received the designation of a "District of Innovation" by the State Department of Education for pioneering efforts in implementing career ladders (tracks) for teachers and for their work on equity. The three tracks include Master Teacher, Teacher Coach, and Teacher Leader.

These tracks were designed to keep quality teachers in the classroom. Reduced loads were assigned to participating teachers to accommodate mentoring and coaching for new, novice, and struggling teachers. The career tracks provide monetary incentives comparable to entry-level administrators and central office personnel.

Mrs. Watson is a veteran elementary teacher and is a candidate for the Teacher Coach track. She is a highly respected member of the staff with nearly thirty years of experience, and she often claims to "have seen it all." Recently, she has become angry—almost to the point of being combative—about the new teacher evaluation systems that have been put in place by the district.

Her frustration is compounded by the fact that the demographics of the district have changed significantly during her long tenure. Like most of her colleagues, 40 to 50 percent of her students are identified as English language learners.

Mrs. Watson has been very vocal that it is unfair she has "those kids" in her classroom because they are "bringing down her test scores." She is resentful and claims her teacher evaluation is invalid because it does not reflect her true teaching abilities, due to the English language learners in her class. She was overheard in the faculty lounge as saying, "They need to learn to speak English. It's not my job to speak Spanish or Arabic."

As principal, what do you do?

_____
_____
_____
_____

SUGGESTED READING: Maulding Green, W., and Leonard, E. *The Soft Skills of Leadership: Navigating with Confidence and Humility*, second edition. Lanham, MD: Rowman & Littlefield, 2019, chapter 6.

ADDITIONAL SELECTED READINGS: Chen, H., and Yuan, Y. "The Study of the Relationships of Teacher's Creative Teaching, Imagination, and Principal's Visionary Leadership." *SAGE Open* 11, no. 3 (2021).

Thinking Outside the Box

Society views career technical education (CTE) simply as Vo-Tech, an elective course for students who will never go to college. Many times, district administrators, with the exception of CTE administrators, do not realize the powerful impact of CTE programs. CTE programs are also state tested like many academic courses.

These tests determine if the state allows the program to remain in that district and/or if the program instructor can continue to teach the program. These programs are vital to the community and provide a foundation for students attending post-secondary schools as well.

Support of CTE by business and industry is an integral part of a successful CTE program. Recruitment and selection of students for these programs must be student-driven. When students choose to take a CTE class, they tend to put forth maximum effort affecting overall accountability ratings for the school district.

The district special education director and assistant director meet with the CTE administrator, requesting that additional special education students are added to CTE programs. As the CTE administrator, you understand the value of CTE programs for special education students. CTE programs are important for all students, especially those who are not going to college or who may struggle just to graduate.

Due to the Carl Perkins legislation, no more than fifteen students may be accepted per block in CTE. Therefore, on a block schedule, forty-five students, maximum, are admitted per program and one of those blocks is designated for second-year students. With thirty spots available for first-year students, depending on program popularity, a great deal of middle- to lower-performing students are not selected.

Allowing student access to CTE is highly beneficial. CTE programs provide national industry certifications that are utilized by business/industry in every state. Access to these programs could be life changing for many of the program students. If students are not given a purpose, they may be lost to dropout or lack of direction in life.

What do you do about the request for more special education students in the CTE program?

_____
_____
_____
_____

SUGGESTED READING: Maulding Green, W., and Leonard, E. *The Soft Skills of Leadership: Navigating with Confidence and Humility*, second edition. Lanham, MD: Rowman & Littlefield, 2019, chapter 6.

ADDITIONAL SELECTED READINGS: Farmer, Y. "Prudence, Ethics and Anticipation in Visionary Leaders." *The Journal of Values-Based Leadership* 15, no. 1 (2022).

CONTRIBUTING AUTHOR'S OPTIONS FOR VISION SITUATIONAL JUDGMENT TESTS

Late Night Call

    A. Tell her not to worry it is just a prank. Get some sleep and be at work tomorrow.
    B. Tell her you will cancel school for tomorrow.
    C. Tell her you are going to contact the superintendent and the local authorities, and you will be back in contact with her after you speak to them.

D. Tell her to post a message on Facebook that your school will be in session tomorrow and that prank messages will not be tolerated.

Digital Tracking

A. Prepare a statement informing the local community that a district employee has been arrested and charged with possession of child pornography and that no further statements will be made by the district while the investigation is underway.
B. Wait out the situation to see what the local authorities have to say.
C. Allow the principal at the school of the offender to handle the situation and communicate with the public.
D. Prepare a statement that puts a clear distance between the employee and the school district while admitting no details of the issue.
E. State "no comment" when asked by the public and media for information about the arrest.

FaceTime

A. Notify the parent(s) again of the student's defiance and warn them that any future incidents of defiance and the student will be suspended from school.
B. Verbally reprimand the student.
C. Call for the basketball coach to arrange an intervention with the student and parent(s).
D. Start proceedings for expulsion from school.
E. Arrange for the student to return to the high school.
F. Suspend the student from alternative school for ten days.

Missing in Action

A. Secure a qualified substitute and assign the department head and instructional coach to help with grading work for the students.
B. Secure a qualified substitute and have the department head prepare the lessons for the remaining days of school. Assign the department head and instructional coach to help with grading work for the students. In fairness to the students, drop the four lowest grades for each student and allow them to turn in work for which they had previously received a zero for not turning in on time during the last two weeks.
C. Secure a qualified substitute and assign the department head and instructional coach to help with grading ongoing work for the students but leave the existing student grades as they are.

D. Rotate the department chair, instructional coach, and other available teachers into the class to cover the remaining school days. Assign the department head and instructional coach to help with grading work for the students and determining final grades.

Savvy School Counselor

A. Leave her alone and hope for the best. She mentions retiring on a regular basis, and you are afraid that she will retire, and then you will have no one to replace her.
B. Initiate an action plan for her. You are tired of her laziness and if she retires, then that's fine.
C. Have a private conversation with her and tell her that you have every confidence that she can do better. Discuss the importance of her role in student learning and success at your school.
D. Call the district office and complain about her to the school counseling supervisor. Maybe he will have a better idea.

Does All Really Mean All?

A. Provide professional learning on cultural competence and the implications for teaching in the twenty-first century.
B. Speak with Mrs. Watson about the "alleged comment" overheard in the faculty lounge.
C. Debrief with Mrs. Watson about her evaluation and offer recommendations for improvements.
D. Address misconceptions regarding the career tracks that are being implemented across the district.

Thinking Outside the Box

A. As director of CTE, you understand CTE programs have to meet Perkins and academic requirements. If a student does not meet certain criteria, they cannot take the course.
B. As director of CTE, working with your instructors, you arrange for special education students to come shadow classes during the school year to gain some experience.
C. As director of CTE, you ask the district for a special education position to work with your CTE counselor and Student Services. You create a new program for special education students.

D. As director of CTE, you request the district provide for a special education position. Working with your CTE counselor and Student Services, you create a program for special education students.

Chapter 6

Lessons on Emotional Intelligence/Soft Skills

Being emotionally intelligent means a lot of things. It includes the ability to recognize emotions in ourselves, controlling or regulating those emotions, acknowledging the same in others, and having social/relationship awareness—this last point is currently commonly referred to as "soft skills."

Additionally, with the incredible influx of technology into our lives, many of us are not nearly as in tune with others as in the past. It is critical, now more than ever in our rapidly advancing, fast-paced society, that we give top priority to this crucial relationship-building and -sustaining skill. Regarding emotional intelligence and the subsequent soft skills therein, we must ask: does the leader say what they mean and support that with their actions? The answer to that question defines the soft skills of the leader.

The scenarios in this chapter are, in one way or another, related to a leader's emotional intelligence/soft skills. If your Leader Acumen Assessment scores indicated this as an area for needed growth, you should work through the scenarios with a couple of things in mind. First, as you work through the scenarios in the chapter take particular note of the "Contributing Authors' Options" to each problem at the end of each chapter of situational judgment tests.

In working through the scenarios and reviewing the "Contributing Authors' Options," one of two things will happen. You will find disparity between your responses and the authors, or you might, indeed, find that your responses coincide with the authors' (see appendix B for a graphic representation). Next, reflect on the information you gained from the Leader Acumen Assessment. If you acknowledge that emotional intelligence/soft skills is an area for growth based on the assessment, ask yourself if this was based on your self-assessment, the CIRCLE assessment, or both.

If either or both assessments (the self or CIRCLE) indicate that you have room for improvement in the area of leader emotional intelligence/soft skills *and* you are also finding disparity in yours and the "Contributing Authors' Options," chances are you will find growth via working through these exercises and accompanying readings.

However, be reminded that this will not happen overnight. Growing your leader acumen is a worthy endeavor but is a painstakingly time-consuming undertaking. It requires rewiring of your thought processes regarding learnings that are very ingrained into your most innate understandings, and this takes time. (See appendix B for a graphic representation.)

On the other hand, if you find your solutions and the solutions offered in the "Contributing Authors' Options" coincide highly, yet your self score is lower than the mean shown at the end of your Leader Acumen Assessment for emotional intelligence/soft skills, one of two things is happening. Either you are lacking in self-confidence, yet your decision making is solid, or conversely, perhaps you are somewhat overconfident, but nonetheless making good decisions.

If the first is the case, working through the scenarios should enhance your self-confidence. The second option (overconfidence) is the one to be most wary of. Leaders in this category often find themselves derailed as leaders, even though they generally are good decision makers. Working through the scenarios should help to instill the idea that there is more than one acceptable solution to most problems/issues and thus lessen one potential major consequence of overconfidence, feeling that you have the only viable solution.

If you opt to have a CIRLE/360-assessment done and find that your solutions and the solutions offered in the "Contributing Authors' Options" coincide highly, yet your CIRCLE scores were outside the standard deviation (available from the Leader Acumen Team when a CIRCLE/360-assessment is done) for emotional intelligence/soft skills, it is possible that a different set of problems is occurring.

Either you are selecting the course of action you believe is best for the scenario, yet in reality you would not implement it, *or* the problem may be one of perception. It is much more likely that it is the former. Only in rare instances would the latter be the case. However, we insert it here for thought because, on occasion, it is the case. And, as the old saying goes: perception is reality.

Perhaps you have indeed highly honed soft skills, yet perception is the issue for your low scores in emotional intelligence/soft skills. This could be a case of projection. For example, you may not seem emotionally intelligent and perhaps for legitimate reasons. You will recall from the chapter on credibility in *The Soft Skills of Leadership: Navigating with Confidence and Humility*, second edition,[1] that mention was made of how "what you wear" infers or projects an image. Such could be the case in this instance.

Finally, improving your leader acumen and "adaptive capacity," as stated in the preface, is a process. As you will recall, the notion of leader acumen is predicated on the theory that there is a genetic predisposition toward leadership.

As Marquis and Tilcsik[2] so aptly noted, imprinting may take place during brief sensitive periods of high susceptibility during the formative process, during the teachable moment, or another yet different time of susceptibility, and that imprints once established are persistent. The lessons in this book are to be utilized to grow leader acumen in this third way—over the long, repetitive process. To that end and to truly be imprinted with any of the competencies, actions for building the various skillsets may be found in appendix C.

The leader who, through developing his/her leader acumen, can also master the ability to recognize and react appropriately to both the rational and emotional sides of an individual have a decided advantage over the leader who lacks those abilities.

EMOTIONAL INTELLIGENCE/SOFT SKILLS SITUATIONAL JUDGMENT TESTS

A Moral Dilemma

On a normal school day, Charity, a mother of a student, asks to speak to you as principal. Charity, who is a well-known nurse practitioner at the local hospital, tells you that her daughter, Lindsey, is struggling with a group of her friends. Charity goes into detail that she just learned that her daughter was raped three months ago by a fellow tenth grader at a back-to-school party after she got drunk and passed out.

Apparently, Lindsey's cheerleader friends are making fun of her about it because another boyfriend/girlfriend couple watched it take place and told everyone. The party in which Lindsey got drunk was thrown by the son of a school board member, and that school board member and her husband reportedly supplied the alcohol.

Charity tells you that she has Lindsey seeing a counselor, but Charity wanted to let you know in case you happened to see students harassing Lindsey. Charity stated she did not want to press charges and has not spoken to the police. Charity is very explicit that she does not want any other adults to know because of how small a community it is, and she doesn't want people gossiping.

What do you do?

SUGGESTED READING: Maulding Green, W., and Leonard, E. *The Soft Skills of Leadership: Navigating with Confidence and Humility*, second edition. Lanham, MD: Rowman & Littlefield, 2019, chapter 7.

ADDITIONAL SELECTED READINGS: Kaur, N., and Hirudayaraj, M. "The Role of Leader Emotional Intelligence in Organizational Learning: A Literature Review Using EI Framework." *New Horizons in Adult Education & Human Resource Development* 33, no. 1 (2021): 51–68.

Family First

Living in an area that relies heavily on immigrant workers for employment, your school district deals with the hardships that often follow families that migrate for employment opportunities. Several of the students who populate your school are children of migrant workers and are many times forced to miss school to work.

As a school leader, it is imperative to be compassionate and prudent in making decisions that will affect the students, their families, their education, and the community at large. The decisions made during these transitional periods have the potential to have a lasting effect.

Juan is a straight A student who rarely misses school. He is very conscientious of his academics and puts forth great effort to maintain excellent grades as well as appropriate behavior at school. His mother came to the school late on a Friday to inform the administration that the father had made the difficult decision to take the family to California for the last three weeks of December to explore employment opportunities. They would be leaving that afternoon.

The mother was concerned because this decision did not allow Juan to take any of his semester exams early or finish any work for the semester. Realizing the importance of Juan's education, the mother shared that she could appeal to the father to postpone the trip so that Juan could complete his assignments on Monday if given the opportunity to finish then.

Realizing the importance of the family staying together, the school leader determined to approach the teachers.

What would you do?

SUGGESTED READING: Maulding Green, W., and Leonard, E. *The Soft Skills of Leadership: Navigating with Confidence and Humility*, second edition. Lanham, MD: Rowman & Littlefield, 2019, chapter 7.

ADDITIONAL SELECTED READINGS: Görgens-Ekermans, G., and Roux, C. "Revisiting the Emotional Intelligence and Transformational Leadership Debate: (How) Does Emotional Intelligence Matter to Effective Leadership?" *South African Journal of Human Resource Management* 19, no. 1 (2021): 1–13.

Gut Punch

A teacher calls you (as principal) to her classroom. The teacher explains that one of her students, from an earlier class, appeared to be agitated. The teacher asked the student what was wrong. The student reported that during her class, another student had hit him in the stomach and knocked the wind out of him. The teacher did not witness this incident.

Three girls who were around the incident were interviewed. The girls said that the boy who punched the student in the stomach was teasing the victim. The victim had tried to get his colored pencils back from the aggressor. His hand brushed up against the aggressor in his attempt to get his colored pencils. This resulted in the aggressor punching the victim in the stomach. The aggressive student admitted to punching the student and downplayed that he took the student's colored pencils. He also revealed that both students are friends.

What do you do?

_____
_____
_____
_____

SUGGESTED READING: Maulding Green, W., and Leonard, E. *The Soft Skills of Leadership: Navigating with Confidence and Humility*, second edition. Lanham, MD: Rowman & Littlefield, 2019, chapter 7.

ADDITIONAL SELECTED READINGS: Gomez-Leal, R., Holzer, A., Bradley, C., Fernandez-Berrocal, P., and Patti, J. "The Relationship between Emotional Intelligence and Leadership in School Leaders: A Systematic Review." *Cambridge Journal of Education* 52, no. 1 (2022): 84.

Picture This

Losing a student to death by suicide is quite possibly one of the hardest tragedies for which a school community must heal. The effects from such an incident will have lasting effects on the students, faculty, family, and community. It is imperative that school leaders provide the necessary support for all those involved and be as transparent as possible when discussing issues relating to such a tragic event.

The decisions made concerning the loss of life are vital in the healing process and should be handled with utmost care and concern for all those involved. Genuine concern should be displayed along with the necessary mental support for all those involved in order for the students to try and process a loss of this magnitude.

Nathan, a seventh-grade band student, tragically died of suicide at home soon after speaking to several of his close friends from school. By the time the students reached out to his parents with concerns, it was too late and his life was over. The visitation and funeral for Nathan was attended by students, faculty, and staff from the school, and the show of support was very comforting to his family.

The students participated in a balloon release in order to honor their friend, and they chose to invite his parents and family to attend this celebration of his life. The school offered mental support, group therapy, and counseling for the weeks and months that followed. Toward the end of the year, when school annuals were delivered, it was immediately discovered that Nathan did not have a school picture in the book.

It was discovered that he had missed due to illness on the original school picture day. The absence of his picture in the annual caused grief among a large portion of the students in his grade.

What would you do?

_____
_____
_____
_____

SUGGESTED READING: Maulding Green, W., and Leonard, E. *The Soft Skills of Leadership: Navigating with Confidence and Humility*, second edition. Lanham, MD: Rowman & Littlefield, 2019, chapter 7.

ADDITIONAL SELECTED READINGS: Cui, Y. "The Role of Emotional Intelligence in Workplace Transparency and Open Communication." *Aggression and Violent Behavior* (March 2021).

Trying Times

An eleventh-grade student lost his father less than two months ago to a drowning accident. The student is trying to help take care of his mother and two younger brothers, as he is now the oldest male in a family of four. The student had been in some trouble at school earlier in the school year, but nothing major. It is now the second quarter of the school year (November, to be exact) and some issues have arisen in the local community, specifically an increase in drug-related problems. The local police are diligently working to ensure the community is a safe place to live.

The student's younger brother, who attends the feeder middle school, was jumped by a twenty-year-old male on the way home from school, while his brother was at the high school at extended day tutoring. The twenty-year-old male told the middle school student he would kill him if he told anyone. Nonetheless, the middle school student told his older brother.

The eleventh-grade student got a forty-five-caliber handgun, loaded it, and promised his younger brother he would protect him from this man. The next morning, he walked his younger brother to the middle school and then continued to the high school to begin his day. As he was running toward his first-period class so he would not be late, the gun fell out of his pocket and one of his peers saw the gun hit the ground in the hallway.

The student who dropped the gun picked it up and continued running toward his first-period class. The incident was reported to you (the assistant principal) by a student.

What do you do?

_____
_____
_____
_____

SUGGESTED READING: Maulding Green, W., and Leonard, E. *The Soft Skills of Leadership: Navigating with Confidence and Humility*, second edition. Lanham, MD: Rowman & Littlefield, 2019, chapter 7.

ADDITIONAL SELECTED READINGS: Miao, C., Humphrey, R., and Qian, S. "Emotional Intelligence and Servant Leadership: A Meta-analytic Review." *Business Ethics: A European Review* 30, no. 2 (2021): 231–43.

Home Away from Home

Teachers work tremendously hard and are rarely, if ever, compensated to the level that they truly deserve. Sometimes, this reality can become a catalyst for questionable behavior. One teacher had a particularly difficult time managing his family logistics. After lining up a new teaching position an hour and a half away, he and his family decided to move. This new location was much closer to his wife's parents and was a vacation spot for many—an ideal area for retirement, which this teacher was close to pursuing.

Once the move was finalized and the family transitioned to their new city, the job that was unofficially promised to this teacher fell through. Additionally, circumstances arose that prevented the teacher from retiring soon, as he had anticipated he would be able to do.

This teacher was a bus driver, a coach, taught multiple preps, and now had to drive an hour and a half to work every day. The school administrative team was informed that he would not be leaving his position, and they were assured that his "home" move would not interfere with his teaching performance.

In fact, they were told that this commute would be some much needed "alone time" where the teacher could use to prepare for the school day on the way to school and unwind on the way home. A month goes by, and administrators notice that this teacher is signing up to work athletic gates (teachers are compensated for this extra time). Although they think it is strange behavior considering he never used to sign up for gates, they dismissed it.

One assistant principal noticed the teacher in the stands by himself during a softball game. This was curious since the teacher had his long drive home and would have to leave early the next morning. The administrator inquired, and the teacher shared that he couldn't take the drive always, so he got a hotel a few nights each week to make the long-distance living situation more tolerable.

The administrators continued to see this teacher at almost every event and would often see him making copies late in the evenings. After checking the school cameras, it was discovered that the teacher was spending the night at school and using the athletic locker rooms to shower.

What do you do?

_____
_____
_____

SUGGESTED READING: Maulding Green, W., and Leonard, E. *The Soft Skills of Leadership: Navigating with Confidence and Humility*, second edition. Lanham, MD: Rowman & Littlefield, 2019, chapter 7.

ADDITIONAL SELECTED READINGS: Vodianoi, M. "How Does Emotional Intelligence Really Help Leaders Succeed?" *Leadership Excellence* 38, no. 11 (2021): 18–20.

Can't Bear It

In the world of public education, students will often conduct themselves in ways that may be puzzling for the adults in the building. While it is not our job to judge behaviors that we find odd, it is our obligation to be observant. Sometimes, although actions might seem innocent, there may be malicious or dangerous motives behind the issue at hand.

The school administration has noticed that a growing number of students, particularly from the theatre club, are carrying around plush stuffed animals at school. Although unusual, there are no rules against stuffed animals, and no harm seems to be coming from their attendance. The theatre students are a close-knit group of students and will often stick with each other, so the behavior was considered normal for group inclusion.

All of these stuffed animals were about the size of a basketball, and the students got to the point where they would keep them on their desks. One day, a teacher texted a school administrator that she thought she saw a student cutting herself in class. The administrator immediately responded and brought the student to the front office for search. Nothing was found on her person or in her bag.

One of the assistant principals, with tears in her eyes, had a heartfelt conversation with the student and told her that she would be devastated if something happened to the student. The girl began to cry and reached for her stuffed bear. She pulled one of the ears back to show a slit that was made in the fabric. She reached in and pulled out a razor blade.

However, this student did not suggest that any of her friends might also be self-harming or using stuffed animals to smuggle other items that could be dangerous.

Considering there were probably ten other students with stuffed animals, what do you do?

_____
_____
_____

SUGGESTED READING: Maulding Green, W., and Leonard, E. *The Soft Skills of Leadership: Navigating with Confidence and Humility*, second edition. Lanham, MD: Rowman & Littlefield, 2019, chapter 7.

ADDITIONAL SELECTED READINGS: Alam, J., and Zaheer, M. "Impact of Empowering Leadership on Employee Burnout: Moderating Role of Emotional Intelligence." *Journal of Managerial Sciences* 15 (July 2021): 98–113.

Chip

You are reviewing emails upon returning to your office and learn that a male student had a chipped tooth because of a metal water bottle hitting it. You immediately go find your school nurse to understand the matter better. She confirms that a student did come in with a chipped tooth. She describes it as barely noticeable, but a chip just the same.

She states that the student was assessed, report made, and the parent contacted. You call the student in to hear his version as to what has happened. The student shares that he was trying to shake a piece of ice out of his metal water bottle. A female student saw him trying to shake the ice into his mouth and tapped the bottom of the bottle. The tapping caused the bottle to hit his bottom tooth, causing it to chip.

The student felt like the whole thing was an accident and that his classmate did not mean it. You call the female student, and she tells the same story. After speaking to both students, you make a call to the parent.

The parent is irate and wants to know who will pay for the dental expenses for her child. She states she is prepared to go to the district office. You tell her you understand her concern and will contact the district office. The parent (the student's mother) makes an appointment to see you the next day to learn of options. When the parent comes in, she comes with the cost of care plan for the tooth and states the tooth is now loose.

What should you do?

_____
_____
_____
_____

SUGGESTED READING: Maulding Green, W., and Leonard, E. *The Soft Skills of Leadership: Navigating with Confidence and Humility*, second edition. Lanham, MD: Rowman & Littlefield, 2019, chapter 7.

ADDITIONAL SELECTED READINGS: Goleman, D. "Leadership Blindspots."*Leader to Leader* 100 (2021): 22–25.

The Request

Suzie is a fourteen-year-old eighth grader. She is popular among the student body and the teachers like her. She has a difficult background and lacks parental support due to the fact that she is from a single-parent household with four other siblings. She is the baby of the family. The parent and the older siblings have had run-ins with the law, and Suzie decided to take a different path in middle school.

She is on the honor roll and has made the basketball team. She is excited for the school year. Early in the fall, she reported to the school nurse that she wasn't feeling good and a lot of the usual school "bugs" were going around. The nurse tried to reach the parent to no avail and told Suzie if she didn't feel better by the end of the weekend to go to the doctor.

In the next couple weeks, the administrator noticed some changes in Suzie and talked to her with the counselor. She reported that she was just tired from basketball. The counselor then attempted to reach the parent. The attempts were unsuccessful.

After the semester holidays, a student confided in the administration that she believed Suzie was pregnant. The administrators were concerned and then also noticed a drop in Suzie's grades. Basketball season was about to begin again.

The administrator and the counselor called Suzie in and told her it was reported that she was pregnant. She admitted that she was indeed pregnant. She was informed she would not be allowed to play basketball because it was dangerous given her condition. She was encouraged to have a conversation with her parents and go to the doctor.

Suzie does as asked and then she tells her teachers and friends. It's all a buzz around campus. The parent wants to have a baby shower at the church and wants to send invitations to her friends and teachers. The student wants to pass them out at the school. The baby shower is in a couple months, and she will miss the first couple weeks of the next school year.

The teachers want to collect money and attend the shower.

What do you do?

_____
_____
_____
_____

SUGGESTED READING: Maulding Green, W., and Leonard, E. *The Soft Skills of Leadership: Navigating with Confidence and Humility*, second edition. Lanham, MD: Rowman & Littlefield, 2019, chapter 7.

ADDITIONAL SELECTED READINGS: Pellitteri, J. "Emotional Intelligence and Leadership Styles in Education." *Psychology & Its Contexts* 12, no. 2 (2021): 39–52.

CONTRIBUTING AUTHORS' OPTIONS FOR EMOTIONAL INTELLIGENCE SITUATIONAL JUDGMENT TESTS

A Moral Dilemma

A. Having been told of the situation and with a mandatory reporting requirement, you tell Charity that you must report what she has shared but that beyond that you will monitor the situation and notify other administrators so that they can be on the lookout for any issues. You also ask Charity if she would like for any of the guidance counselors to speak to Lindsey and/or set up a safe place where Lindsay can go to speak to someone.

B. Having been told of the situation and with a mandatory reporting requirement, you tell Charity that you must report what she has shared but to make sure you also ask Charity if you understood correctly that she had not notified law enforcement or the Department of Human Resources.

C. Having been told of the situation and with a mandatory reporting requirement, you tell Charity that you must report what she has shared and end the conversation at that point.

D. Having been told of the situation and with a mandatory reporting requirement, you tell Charity that you must report what she has shared. Per accepted procedure, you notify your superintendent of the report and potential board member issues.

Family First

A. Put Juan's education first and ask the parents to postpone the employment opportunity trip to California.

B. Allow Juan to go but put zeros in for all missing tasks. His grades are good enough that he would still pass his classes. The family could stay together and go to California as planned.

C. Allow the teachers to exempt Juan from his remaining class assignments and exams.

D. Give Juan incompletes for all assignments he is missing and allow him to make them up if he returns and they do not take employment in California.

E. Teachers would exempt Juan from the last few assignments and exams since his grades, behavior, and attendance would allow this exemption if all his classes were semester classes. This would allow Juan to take exams when and if he returns for the sole purpose of remediation and data for future instruction.

Gut Punch

A. Contact the parents of both students and inform them of the incident. Warn them that the next time an incident occurs, both students will be suspended from school.
B. Interview both students about the incident.
C. Suspend both students out of school for fighting.
D. Discipline the aggressive student only.
E. Ignore the incident as boys playing rough.
F. Seek the advice of both parents on what to do.

Picture This

A. Make no mention of the absence of a picture of Nathan and hope that the students will get over it quickly.
B. Get a picture from Nathan's parents, make copies for the students, and pass it out to them at school.
C. Ask to have the annual recopied for the seventh grade with Nathan's picture added.
D. Be forthcoming about the absence of his picture and tell the students that he will have a memorial page in next year's annual. School leaders could show the students an example of how deceased students have been honored in the annual in the past.
E. Gather the students in an assembly, invite the family, and have school leaders apologize for leaving Nathan's picture out of the annual.

Trying Times

A. Call the police, have the eleventh-grade student arrested, and recommend expulsion from school.
B. Get the student to your office, investigate the incident, and determine if he truly has a weapon in his possession. Take the weapon, dispose of it, and send him back to class.
C. Get the student to your office, investigate the incident, and determine why he has a weapon on campus. Notify the principal and resource officer to investigate the incident with you and ensure the school is locked down. Recommend alternative placement school for the student to continue his education in a different setting.

D. Place the school on lockdown, get the student to your office, investigate the incident, call the police, and have the student arrested and immediately kick him out of school.
E. Place the school on lockdown, notify the resource officer, call the police, and let them oversee the matter.

Home Away from Home

A. Let him continue this arrangement—he isn't hurting anyone or anything and having the additional support during extracurricular activities is a huge help.
B. Address the faculty as a whole about people taking advantage of taxpayer-funded resources.
C. Have a conversation with the teacher and tell him that he is not allowed to live at school.
D. Get with human resources (HR) and pursue termination of said employee for using publicly funded resources for personal use.

Can't Bear It

A. Call the parents of these students.
B. Address the theatre students when they have theatre class.
C. Ban all stuffed animals from campus.
D. All of the above.

Chip

A. You contact the insurance and liability office for the district to cover the dental bill.
B. You tell Mom the bill is hers to address and that the school district will not be involved.
C. You contact the parent of the female student, make her aware of the incident, and that the other party will be in touch with a dental bill.
D. Put both parents in touch with each other to work out payment of the bill.

The Request

A. Monitor and accommodate the student with a table instead of a student desk, but take no action regarding the baby shower and invitation delivery.
B. Let the student pass out the invitations at the school.

C. Tell the parent the invitations must be mailed to the student's invitees instead of handing them out at school.
D. Tell the teachers they can, at their discretion, give the parent a gift card but discourage them from attending the shower. The gift card cannot be on behalf of the school.
E. Stay in contact with the parent and wait until the family can decide what is best for the baby.

Chapter 7

Contributing Authors' Solutions for Situational Judgment Tests

Disclaimer:

On the following pages are the contributing authors' recommended solutions, rationale for the recommended solution, and rationale for rejection of alternative solutions. These recommendations are in no way intended to supersede work policy or act as legal advice to the learner. These are actual situations encountered by the contributing authors, including the solutions they enacted at the time and place of the circumstance.

CREDIBILITY

Contributing Authors' Solutions

Snacks, Anyone?

Best Response—D: Reprimand the teacher for not following the school and district policy concerning collection of money.
Rationale for the Best Response: Teachers are given the teacher handbook at the beginning of the year, and one of the key points covered is the collection of money and how it must be turned into the school bookkeeper. The teacher totally disregarded this policy. Upon further investigation, it was ascertained that this teacher was purchasing alcoholic beverages with the money from the snack cart. Many times, where there is smoke, there is fire.
Rationale for Rejecting the Alternate Responses:

A. A possible first step but one that does not fully address the issue.
B. Another possible first step, but again one that does not fully address the issue.
C. Looking the other way simply makes you complicit in the wrongdoing. As the principal, you have an obligation to enforce policy.

Mad Texting

Best Response—C: Interview the students, determine if there are any others involved, then suspend the students for a period prescribed by policy.
Rationale for the Best Response: Social media is one of an administrator's biggest headaches. But unlike face-to-face confrontations, social media leaves a trail of evidence. In this situation, the infraction occurred off campus, but the issue had the potential to carry onto the school campus. By taking decisive action, future incidents will be deterred.
Rationale for Rejecting the Alternate Responses:

A. This option is possible, but a firmer stance will send a message to these students as well as others.
B. This option is not strong enough. Students may be inclined to continue online threats.
D. This is an option, but again may not allow for enough separation from the incidents.
E. This is an option, but again may not allow for enough separation from the incidents.
F. This becomes a police matter only if parents submit a complaint with the police. If this were to have happened on campus, then administration would report the threats to the police.

Peek-a-Boo

Best Response—F: Suspend the student for five days.
Rationale for the Best Response: This is an interesting case. Although the best response would be out-of-school suspension, in this case, the student was actually assigned to the alternative school for forty-five days because of the administrator's verbal threat being ignored. Prior to this incident, this student had only one minor disciplinary infraction. The student was emotionally distraught on this day. A teacher she did not have was yelling at her. She made the decision to walk away to avoid saying something wrong, an act of defiance. Furthermore, she refused to follow the instructions of the administrator, also an act of defiance. But with no serious priors, would this incident warrant sending a student to the alternative school? This action tells the student that they are on the verge of being expelled. Is the administrator obligated to send

the student to the alternative because they said they would? Suspending the student for five days sends the right message.
Rationale for Rejecting the Alternate Responses:

A. This option is possible, but with the act of defiance toward the administrator the situation calls for stronger measures.
B. This option is not strong enough.
C. This is an option that must occur to determine why the student chose her actions. But this is not the only action to be taken.
D. This action is extreme. This action should be reserved for the most egregious conduct.
E. Defiance is a serious infraction; a student who openly defies authority within the school must deal with more severe consequences than in-school suspension.

The Oversharing Employee

Best Responses—B and C: You ask the employee to delete the post from her Facebook page. You address the employee regarding being on campus after her scheduled time.
Rationale for the Best Responses: While a personal post like this is not a violation of the district's Acceptable Use policy, it has the potential to cause issues at school. When social media posts not made at school cause interruptions at school, they must be addressed. The employee is sharing information about the school and in some way is acting as a representative of the school by sharing. A discussion about being on campus before/after scheduled time needs to also be addressed. This can lead to overtime issues and liability issues if she were to get hurt.
Rationale for Rejecting the Alternate Responses:

A. You can't ignore the actions taken. At the very least, a documented conversation needs to occur.

Upgrade Complaints

Best Response—B: You ask for written statements from both employees and have a conversation with the technology director about next steps.
Rationale for the Best Response: The issue needs to be addressed. The technology department director must be included, since their employee is also involved. You do not have the authority (if needed) to discipline someone

else's employee. It is always best to get everything in writing. This way, the issues addressed in the statement are all handled.
Rationale for Rejecting the Alternate Responses:

A. You cannot ignore the complaint.
C. You don't have the authorization to write up an employee from another department.
D. While a reassignment may occur after you take statements and discuss the situation with the technology director, you don't want to start with that request without any facts.

Sticky Situation

Best Response—C: Discipline the teacher according to Code of Ethics and AUP Violation, and discipline the student according to handbook policy, notifying the parent of the student's consequence.
Rationale for the Best Response: Both the student and the teacher were appropriately trained on the Acceptable Use policy. The teacher was also trained on the Code of Ethics. The teacher violated the AUP and the Code of Ethics by acting unprofessionally. Both the student and the teacher should be disciplined based on district policy. However, the disciplinary action taken with the teacher is a confidential personnel matter.
Rationale for Rejecting the Alternate Responses:

A. The student is not the only one who should receive consequences; the teacher should have been more responsible.
B. The incident requires more than a discussion for both the teacher and the student.
D. This could be an additional option in conjunction with C, but more should be done than suspension of use.

Duck, Duck, Goose

Best Response—D: Expel the student.
Rationale for the Best Response: As heartbreaking as this consequence is, it is the consistent consequence to bringing firearms on campus. If it became known that we were lenient with this student because we liked him, then every other instance would be questioned. There can't be any toleration for guns on campus.
Rationale for Rejecting the Alternate Responses:

A. A potential first step, but it leaves the situation unresolved.

B. Also, a potential step and one that merits strong consideration given the circumstance but fails to follow policy.
C. Again, a potential step but one that does not address policy.

Graduation Is Finally Here!

Best Response—C: Contact the superintendent to find out if the parent's request is within the district's policy. Also, discuss the pros and cons of allowing Jackson to participate in the ceremony. Seek their advice and support.
Rationale for the Best Response: You should always contact the district's superintendent or assistant superintendent before making a decision that may go against the district's policy. It is also essential to make the superintendent aware of the details prior to parents contacting district officials.
Rationale for Rejecting the Alternate Responses:

A. Gives the principal full autonomy but leaves room for the superintendent to override the decision if the parent requests a meeting.
B. Will accommodate Jackson's family but requires more time and planning for your administrative team. In addition, if a private ceremony is held for Jackson's family, you must be willing to consider doing the same for other students in a similar situation in the future.
D. Allowing Jackson to participate in the ceremony without the superintendent's consent could cause you to violate the school district's discipline policy. Jackson's participation could also cause a safety issue for those attending the ceremony.

Rigor or Relationships?

Best Response—C: Stick to the policy.
Rationale for the Best Response: As a school district leader, policy is the only safety net you have. School board policy is also something that you can't just change on whim. Once policy has been voted on by the school board, the only changes that can be made to the policy come by another school board vote. Any attempt by school leadership to circumvent these policies could result in very serious consequences.[1]
Rationale for Rejecting the Alternate Responses:

A. Using friendship to justify a direct intervention is poor practice.
B. If the policy is that onerous, this might be a worthy step but having been in place for two years reduces the likelihood that it is that poorly constructed.
D. Direct intervention oversteps your purview as superintendent.

COMPETENCE

Contributing Authors' Solutions

Inclusive Technology or a Technology No-No?

Best Response—C: As an interim step, take away the computer. Call an individual education plan meeting and, if appropriate, discipline the student as called for by the disciplinary code. Return the computer to the student but only to be used when under the direct supervision of a teacher at school.
Rationale for the Best Response: This allows for a determination of whether the student's action is related to their handicapping condition and on that basis what disciplinary action can be taken. It also allows the student continued use of the computer but with monitored access.
Rationale for Rejecting the Alternate Responses:

A. As principal, you should be involved but as this is a special education student, procedures/guidelines must be followed. Unilateral action (as there is no threat to the student individually or others) is unwarranted.
B. A potentially satisfactory solution but one that places to much responsibility on non-school personnel (the parent).
D. Another potential solution but one that possibly strains the resources of the school and allows the student too much freedom including the possibly of inappropriate use again.
E. As a follow-up to any action taken, this might be a good step but opens the potential for the school to be responsible for psychiatric/psychological treatment.

Student Parking

Best Response—D: Interview the student, then based on the report of the resource officer, send the student to the systems' alternative school per term afforded by district policy.
Rationale for the Best Response: The situation could have gone with a lighter sentence of five days of suspension. The student had no prior incidents with school administration. However, consistency is key in discipline assignment. Inconsistency is remembered by students and parents.
Rationale for Rejecting the Alternate Responses:

A. Parents need to be notified as well as having a face-to-face conference. But a warning is not sufficient.
B. This option is not strong enough.
C. This is an option, but a conference with the parent(s) is also needed.

E. This is an option but may not match the seriousness of the incident.
F. This happened on school property. The police need not be contacted unless there is suspicion of inappropriate conduct (i.e., age related).

Bullying Parent

Best Response—A: Because this problem has gone on for a few months, and you have been unable to remedy the situation, you decide to talk to your supervisor to see what she suggests.
Rationale for the Best Response: You are concerned that the parent's lies about you are affecting the school community's beliefs about your integrity. You have already replied to many of this parent's emails and have spent hours on the phone and meeting face-to-face with her to listen to her many concerns to no avail. At this point, you need advice and support from your supervisor.
Rationale for Rejecting the Alternate Responses:

B. You have tried many times to talk to the mother, but the problem continues to worsen. Therefore, at this point, it's best to discuss the matter with your supervisor.
C. You have ignored some emails and phone calls from this parent with the hope that she will calm down. However, this tactic does not work with this parent. When you ignore her, she only calls or emails again and/or calls the district office.
D. As a leader, you should always rise above the fray. Do *not* get down in the dirt with her—you will get dirty too.

Cleanliness Is a Virtue

Best Response—B: Talk to her again and give her another chance, but now begin documenting.
Rationale for the Best Response: Because finding someone to replace this custodian is unlikely, meet with her again to give her one last chance. It's best to begin documenting your meetings with her and give her a specific schedule and possibly an action plan since there is a strong possibility that she still won't correct the problems.
Rationale for Rejecting the Alternate Responses:

A. Given the fact that it will be difficult to replace the custodian, termination is probably not best in this situation. Perhaps this is the best option at the end of the school year.
C. You do not have time to do the custodian's job. While this solution may be tempting, it is not what is best. Part of your job is to ensure that others do their jobs.

D. It is not fair for the other custodians to take care of her responsibilities.

A Place to Start

Best Response—C: Consider a placement at the district alternative school for a transition period.
Rationale for the Best Response: Brandon is academically and behaviorally far behind his peers and needs a smaller environment to begin to catch up and to learn acceptable behaviors.
Rationale for Rejecting the Alternate Responses:

A. The regular classroom has thirty students and, even with a special education teacher, does not allow for time to work on the reading and behavioral deficits.
B. This should be done but will not solve the immediate problems facing Brandon in the regular classroom.
D. Placing Brandon in a lower grade will only exacerbate the problem. He might totally shut down, and his behavioral issues could be a distraction for the students in that grade.

Hot Head

Best Response—C: Contact the teacher that evening ask him to stay home, conduct a thorough investigation to include statements from witnesses, and contact the superintendent. (In the end, the teacher resigned. He did not fight the last allegation, admitting to using profanity. He offered his resignation, and it was accepted.)
Rationale for the Best Response: Repeated offenses require firm action including termination.
Rationale for Rejecting the Alternate Responses:

A. A good starting point but an incomplete solution.
B. This fails to address the issue and opens the door for future problems.

Christmas Party

Best Response—A: Immediately, put the school on lockdown, turn off all lights, put kids in their safe spot, keep parents in their vehicles, and wait for more information from the police.
Rationale for the Best Response: Safety is most important and having been notified by the police warrants action.

Rationale for Rejecting the Alternate Responses:

    B. While a similar response, this is more intrusive.
    C. Taking no action is inviting disaster.

ABILITY TO INSPIRE

Contributing Authors' Solutions

Guilt by Association?

Best Response—D: Place Darren in alternative school for forty-five days.
Rationale for the Best Response: The student did not bring the gun to school but was obviously aware of the gun, did not report it to school authorities, and actually may have handled the gun. This punishment reflects the severity of his actions.
Rationale for Rejecting the Alternate Responses:

    A. This is too severe, as he did not bring the gun to school.
    B. This is too lenient given his actions.
    C. This might be considered but should be in conjunction with other actions.
    E. This would produce a negative impact when other students found out that Darren was involved but given a pass.

One-to-One: A Blessing or a Curse?

Best Response—C: Text your administrative team, which includes your principal.
Rationale for the Best Response: Notifying the administrative team is imperative. If a response is not received, it would be proper to contact the parents immediately. If no response was received from the parents, notifying the police would logically be the next step.
Rationale for Rejecting the Alternate Responses:

    A. Although this statement may be true, those details need to be worked out ahead of time with the district leaders and the attorney.
    B. Administrators do deserve time with family; however, this situation could become a life-or-death matter and must take priority.
    D. This should be done but does not have to be the first step. If the principal has not responded within a couple of minutes, then the parent should be notified.

E. This would become necessary if the principal and parent have not responded.

Team Spirit

Best Response—B: Allow the student to join the basketball team when he returns to regular school.
Rationale for the Best Response: This student has made a mistake but has served the punishment that was given to him and has had no further discipline problems. He tried out for and made the basketball team on his own, and it is in his best interest to rejoin the team. It will be up to him to make wise choices in order to retain his place on the team according to the team rules and expectations. Giving him this second chance may make a life-altering difference for this student.
Rationale for Rejecting the Alternate Responses:

A. This response is viable but is not what is in the best interest of this student.
C. This is a possible choice, but the student has already served his punishment and not being allowed to play would appear to be further punishment.
D. It is never a wise choice to make an example out of any student.
E. This choice would be possible but would still be considered additional punishment for the student.

The Digital Age

Best Response—C: You contact the student's parents immediately.
Rationale for the Best Response: Even though it is not a school day, you cannot let information about a student's well-being go unchecked. Some may argue that the search did not occur during the school day or time frame, but because you are presented with the information, you cannot just ignore it.
Rationale for Rejecting the Alternate Responses:

A. Doing nothing is not acceptable. You cannot ignore the call for help by the student.
B. While in some situations, this may be appropriate, it is not in this case.
D. Contacting the parents is the best option.

Proselytizing Physical Education Coach

Best Response—D: Have the coach come to your office and talk through the problem. Perhaps it's best to hear his side of the story before making a final decision.

Rationale for the Best Response: This response is best because you need to give the coach a chance to explain the situation. In many cases, students exaggerate a problem to their parents, and when the parents call you, they make accusations that may not be true. As the school leader, you should give your teachers the benefit of the doubt and trust their judgment, unless they give you cause to not trust them. In this case, once you talk to the coach and hear his perspective, you find that he did not have the student write "The Lord's Prayer" at all; he simply talked to the student about the importance of following The Golden Rule.

Rationale for Rejecting the Alternate Responses:

A. It is never wise to ignore a problem. Have the courage to talk to the coach to find out what happened.
B. You know the coach, the student, and the parent best, so calling the physical education supervisor is not best. It will only complicate the matter.
C. It is unfair to the coach to not share the concern with him. While this conversation might be difficult, it is the coach's right to know about this parent's concern.

Donating Sick Days

Best Response—C: Explain to teachers that they are not obligated to donate days and have a conversation with the assistant principal and advise her to stop asking for sick days from the teachers.

Rationale for the Best Response: The assistant principal needs to understand that she is in a position where she should not be making deals with the teachers for days. A fundraiser for days could have been organized if it was needed by others.

Rationale for Rejecting the Alternate Responses:

A. This action addresses one side of the issue but not both.
B. Informing the superintendent is a good idea but not addressing the assistant principal leaves the issues unresolved.

Close to Home

Best Response—B: Now that you are aware that the incidents did happen, you should place the call to Child Protective Services and place the teacher on administrative leave until the investigation is complete.

Rationale for the Best Response: Mrs. Baker as an educator in clear violation of her obligation to report such incidents to the administration as well as to Child Protective Services. Placing her on administrative leave will allow time to investigate without worrying if Mrs. Baker is talking about the situation to other kids or possibly trying to discuss it further with the two students in question. This will also allow you time to share information and gain further direction from your school superintendent, as well as time to speak personally with the student's parents.

Rationale for Rejecting the Alternate Responses:

- A. With knowledge otherwise, this is a non sequitur.
- C. The teacher has already made a serious misstep. Encouraging another misstep is a bad idea.
- D. At some point, a parent conference may be called for but not taking the approach suggested.

Grieving

Best Response—C: As the district leader, you address the staff and student needs face-to-face the next morning.

Rationale for the Best Response: District leadership may not be as close to every situation that happens on each campus, but they are ultimately responsible for making sure that each situation is handled with what is best for students in mind. In this scenario, the best thing for students and staff was to know that their district leadership would be there to support them.

Rationale for Rejecting the Alternate Responses:

- A. District office personnel should be asked to come out for assistance to provide a listening ear or cover a teacher duty for the day. However, asking them to handle the crisis on their own is a failure to lead.
- B. There may be staff that legitimately need to take off. However, it is best for students who will be receiving this news at school to have familiar faces they can talk to and find comfort in.
- D. This should occur. You should ask local pastors, counselors, etc., to come to the campus that morning to counsel with students and staff as needed. However, they are not the face of the district and should not be asked to act alone.

Never Give Up

Best Response—E: Ask the high school to give him a chance to pull the grades up and hold the decision with regard to dropping out until the end of the year. And as director of career technical education (CTE), when Jose is in your facility, have your student services coordinators offer him tutoring so he can get his grades up continue in school.
Rationale for the Best Response: This young man has had it extremely hard. He struggles with the language as well as having to work since seventh grade to help provide for his family. As director of CTE, there is already tutoring available for CTE students as well as support for English language learner students. By providing this service, you know Jose will get the additional support needed and have everything in place to be successful.
Rationale for Rejecting the Alternate Responses:

A. As director of CTE, he is your student.
B. This is a viable option but is not the best solution to get the result needed.
C. This is a viable option but is not the best solution to get the result needed.
D. This option is better than option B but does not give the student a chance to obtain their desired goal.

VISION

Contributing Authors' Solutions

Late Night Call

Best Response—C: Tell her you are going to contact the superintendent and the local authorities, and you will be back in contact with her after you speak to them.[2]
Rationale for the Best Response: Prompt action is required when threats are made.
Rationale for Rejecting the Alternate Responses:

A. Threats are to be taken seriously. This response would not be appropriate.
B. This action without further input would be an overreaction.
D. Perhaps tempting, but it does not address what could be a serious issue.

Digital Tracking

Best Response—A: Prepare a statement informing the local community that a district employee has been arrested and charged with possession of child pornography and that no further statements will be made by the district while the investigation is underway.

Rationale for the Best Response: There is not enough information at the time to know if students are involved in any way or if the employee has broken the law; therefore, the superintendent's statements could impact the case by making a statement that leads the public to a certain assumption. Also, all that you, as superintendent, have shared is public information and available for the media to access. The statement does not divulge privileged information, but it does shut down any future contact from the media and the public while guarding the identity of any students that may be part of an investigation. In this case, the statement effectively stopped any conversation that happened internally as well, which made the continued employment of the parent of the offender a possibility.

Rationale for Rejecting the Alternate Responses:

- B. The story would be out of control within hours of the arrest and the opportunity to lead the narrative would be taken from the superintendent. There would be no "do-overs."
- C. A school principal is not equipped to consider the varied audiences of the district that must be communicated with in this type of situation. The school-level administrator also needs to align with the faculty to preserve trust by the parents of all students. He should not be seen as a bureaucrat but as an advocate for his students.
- D. Any statement that makes room for speculation is a bad place to land. Also, a statement that puts a district on the defensive engenders distrust or implies that the district has something to hide.
- E. No comment is a comment. It can be interpreted as the speaker is not caring about the concerns of parents and the public.

FaceTime

Best Response—D: Start proceedings for expulsion from school.

Rationale for the Best Response: The constant defiance and disrespect toward authority leads to this decision. Multiple previous conferences with the parent have not influenced the student's behavior, despite informing the parent the student was in danger of being expelled.

Rationale for Rejecting the Alternate Responses:

- A. This option should occur, but parents had been conferenced with several times prior to informing them of this potential action.
- B. This action has been done, but in this case, the student has taken the incident to a higher level of infraction.

C. This action had been done several times, with limited success.
E. This action would not have any behavioral consequences.
F. This would be the next option. The student's uncontrollable defiance and disrespect make expulsion a foregone conclusion.

Missing in Action

Best Response—B: Secure a qualified substitute and have the department head prepare the lessons for the remaining days of school. Assign the department head and instructional coach to help with grading work for the students. In fairness to the students, drop the four lowest grades for each student and allow them to turn in work they had received a zero for not turning in on time for the last two weeks.
Rationale for the Best Response: These actions provide the best path forward in fairness to the students.
Rationale for Rejecting the Alternate Responses:

A. A good first step but incomplete.
C. Partially good steps but not addressing the student grading issues is problematic.
D. A potential solution but incomplete.

Savvy School Counselor

Best Response—C: Have a private conversation with her and tell her that you have every confidence that she can do better. Discuss the importance of her role in student learning and success at your school.
Rationale for the Best Response: Because you know that your counselor is capable, and effective school counselors are few and far between, invite the school counselor to your office and have a private conversation with her that is encouraging but also shares your high expectations for her and her school counseling program. Make sure that she understands the importance of her role within the school community and how it impacts student learning and achievement.
Rationale for Rejecting the Alternate Responses:

A. If you leave her alone, the problem will probably get worse, and that is not fair to the students. As the school leader, you must show courage and have a difficult conversation in order to solve the problem.
B. An action plan is too severe of a consequence. You believe that a conversation or two will solve the issue.
D. Calling the district office to complain will not solve the problem. You know your school and your counselor best.

Does All Really Mean All?

Best Response—A: Provide professional learning on cultural competence and the implications for teaching in the twenty-first century.

Rationale for the Best Response: Effective leaders understand that context is key to leadership. Mrs. Watson's issues were indicative of a common trend in twenty-first-century education: changing demographics. It should be noted that in the scenario referenced that Mrs. Watson's classroom demographics were like all of her colleagues. If equity is the goal, then all should mean all. Professional learning is the best vehicle for improvement and is a viable mechanism by which to explore and gain knowledge on what it means to teach with equity and inclusivity.

By carefully outlining the professional development, the principal can address responses B, C, and D through the lens of teaching with equity and how equity serves as a catalyst to higher efficiency and excellence (successful outcomes for all learners).

Rationale for Rejecting the Alternate Responses:

- B. As a standalone option, response B is less favorable, as the principal has received this information secondhand. It also has the potential to strain staff relations and distrust among the staff.
- C. As a leader, you often want to treat the problem not the symptoms. In this case, Mrs. Watson's poor evaluations were symptomatic of a bigger issue: the changing demographics of her classroom. This scenario highlights English language learners but could have applied to any other subgroups such as special education students, low socioeconomic status students, or Black males.
- D. Evaluations are part of the formative feedback cycle and are integral to ensure that the learner engages in continual reflection and growth. The career track allows for customization and authentic interest based professional learning. Coaching requires both a facilitative and instructional skillset. It is through the analysis of one's own practice that teachers come to master the art and science of teaching.

Thinking Outside the Box

Best Response—D: As director of CTE, you request the district provide for a special education position. Working with your CTE counselor and Student Services, you create a program for special education students.

Rationale for the Best Response: Having a special education instructor for CTE is a win-win. There are students with Individualized Education Plans already enrolled in CTE courses, opening courses to students with

Individualized Education Plans and rostering them under the special education instructor will give opportunities to students who really need a pathway after high school. This will fill a need as well for business/industry partners by providing entry-level employees who want to work. By rostering them under a special education instructor, they can sit for any industry certification, but their score will not be included in the official report for Minnesota Department of Education (MDE) and Perkins guidelines. Having a special education instructor in the CTE center would benefit the students with Individualized Education Plans already rostered, providing an added level of support for them when needed.

Rationale for Rejecting the Alternate Responses:

A. If we are truly in it for the students, this is not an option we should choose.
B. A potential step in the right direction but one that does not address the current need. This is the next best solution. However, due to safety training before going into the lab, there is not enough time for them to gain enough experience to go to work.
C. Both potential solutions, but long term do not address the current need.

EMOTIONAL INTELLIGENCE/SOFT SKILLS

Contributing Authors' Solutions

A Moral Dilemma

Best Response—D: Having been told of the situation and with a mandatory reporting requirement, you tell Charity that you must report what she has shared. Per accepted procedure, you notify your superintendent of the report and potential board member issues.

Rationale for the Best Response: You are under a mandatory reporting requirement. You must fulfill that obligation. Accepted procedure is to alert the superintendent of any developing issues.

Rationale for Rejecting the Alternate Responses:

A. A potential step but that is incomplete. This fulfills your mandatory reporting requirement and is empathetic but does not address needed internal communication.
B. A potential step but that is incomplete. This fulfills your mandatory reporting requirement and may move the mother to act but does not address needed internal communication.
C. A potential step but one that leaves the situation unresolved.

Family First

Best Response—E: Teachers would exempt Juan from the last few assignments and exams since his grades, behavior, and attendance would allow this exemption if all his classes were semester classes. This would allow Juan to take exams when and if he returns for the sole purpose of remediation and data for future instruction.

Rationale for the Best Response: Juan has demonstrated his dedication to his studies, behavior, and attendance. His current grades are a good indication that he has mastered the content of his classes. Making the trip with his family would keep the family intact and provide him with stability. School board policy allows for exemptions for certain criteria, which he has met if the class was a semester course. If the family chooses to stay in California for employment, Juan's grades would transfer with validity and as a true reflection of his ability. If they return, Juan could take the exams for remediation and future instructional needs.

Rationale for Rejecting the Alternate Responses:

A. This option could possibly put the family at risk of an employment deficit, which could negatively affect the health and well-being of the entire family.
B. This option would drop Juan's grade averages substantially and would not be a true reflection of his efforts or ability.
C. This option could be chosen, but taking the exam for the sole purpose of remediation and providing data for future instruction would be more beneficial if the move does not occur.
D. This option would work if he did indeed return; however, this option does not consider the possibility that the family might stay in California.

Gut Punch

Best Response—D: Discipline the aggressive student only.

Rationale for the Best Response: This was a pure gut decision, one that you are most likely will have during your tenure. The boys were friends. However, the aggressor was twice the size of the other boy and freely admitted what happened but was insistent that he was punched by the other student. The witnesses said this was not the case. Since the aggressor had no prior discipline issues, he was placed in in-school suspension for two days.[3]

Rationale for Rejecting the Alternate Responses:

A. The parents should be contacted, and this action is an option; however, it was not selected since the aggressor did not have any prior discipline.

B. This should be done as well as applying discipline.
C. This is a possibility, but no priors on either side and a one-sided confrontation weighed in the decision.
E. It is best not to ignore the incident, especially with consideration of the perceived bullying of one student based on the size difference of the two students.
F. This is never an option.

Picture This

Best Response—D: Be forthcoming about the absence of his picture and tell the students that he will have a memorial page in next year's school annual. School leaders could show the students an example of how deceased students have been honored in the annual in the past.
Rationale for the Best Response: Being completely honest and transparent about a difficult situation is always best practice, especially when dealing with such a sensitive subject. The truth that he missed on the day that pictures were taken is reasonable and easy for students to understand. By sharing how students have been memorialized in the past, the school leader would be assuring students that their classmate was valued, loved, and will be remembered.
Rationale for Rejecting the Alternate Responses:

A. Not addressing the concerns of the students is not healthy for them in the healing process.
B. This is an option but does not address the concerns of his picture not being in the school annual.
C. This option would not be financially sound and would not include Nathan's friends from other grades at the school.
E. Although apologizing is a good option, this option even further re-opens the loss and still does not address the students' concern over Nathan's picture not being in the school annual.

Trying Times

Best Response—C: Get the student to your office, investigate the incident, and determine why he has a weapon on campus. Notify the principal and resource officer to investigate the incident with you and ensure the school is locked down. Recommend alternative placement school for the student to continue his education in a different setting.
Rationale for the Best Response: This young man has been through a lot. You have a positive relationship with him and genuinely care about his well-being and that of his family. Nonetheless, you must follow certain

protocols within the district code of conduct and the minimum consequence issued was to recommend for alternative school placement so the student could continue his education. You also wanted to assist the student in understanding the proper way to care for himself and his family. The administrator gave the student an opportunity to continue his education while serving his consequence.

Rationale for Rejecting the Alternate Responses:

A. This option could occur within the scope of the disciplinary infraction of bringing a weapon on campus. However, this is not the best option, as it does not allow the student to continue his education in another setting for up to a calendar year. It also does not warrant the student his rights to due process.
B. This is an unethical response to the scenario and should not be considered. It also does not hold the student accountable for his actions in any way.
D. This option could occur. However, it does not take into account the student's opportunity to continue his education. It also does not take into the account the student's situational history and compassion for what the young man has gone through and his intentions behind the scenario.
E. This option is not completely wrong; however, it does not address what administrators should be doing in accordance with disciplinary actions being issued to ensure a safe and orderly learning environment.

Home Away from Home

Best Response—C: Have a conversation with the teacher and tell him that he is not allowed to live at school.
Rationale for the Best Response: This conversation must take place immediately and must be documented. The ramifications of these decisions must also be discussed. The teacher should sign the minutes of the meeting, and the situation should also be communicated to human resources.
Rationale for Rejecting the Alternate Responses:

A. This allows an undesirable situation to continue.
B. This fails to address the question directly.
D. An overreach for this behavior.

Can't Bear It

Best Response—D: Call the parents of these students. Address the theatre students when they have that class. Ban all stuffed animals from campus.

Rationale for the Best Response: This situation must be handled thoroughly and delicately. We didn't want to bring additional attention to the stuffed animals, which is why we decided to address it with the students in the theatre class. We told them that stuffed animals weren't allowed any longer because we cared about them and found out that some students were using them to bring things to school that they shouldn't. We also called every student's parents to discuss the situation with them and asked that they have a conversation with their children and check the stuffed animals.
Rationale for Rejecting the Alternate Responses:
None, as all options were accepted.

Chip

Best Response—D: Put both parents in touch with each other to work out payment of the bill. The school has no liability, and it is up to the parents to resolve the issue.
Rationale for the Best Response: In the end, under the advisement of the superintendent I put both parents in touch with each other and the bill was satisfied. The superintendent further stated that all campuses needed to do a better job informing parents about supplemental insurance.
Rationale for Rejecting the Alternate Responses:

A. This admits liability and is not a good idea.
B. This is a potential step but does not address the circumstance of the injury.
C. Contacting one party and not the other is a partial solution at best.

The Request

Best Response—D: Stay in contact with the parent and wait until the family can decide what is best for the baby.
Rationale for the Best Response: Situations change, and the well-being of the student and child is the priority. The family could decide to give up the baby for adoption or allow another family to raise the baby. The school should not get involved.
Rationale for Rejecting the Alternate Responses:

A. This option is in the best interest of the student and can be afforded to any student with a medical condition.
B. Birthday party invitations are not allowed to be passed out school per the handbook, and baby shower invitations are no exception.
C. Explain that invitations must be mailed to the students/parents just like birthday invitations per the handbook.

E. Explain to the teachers that the school staff doesn't attend birthday parties of the students, and the school isn't going to set a precedent by attending the baby shower and giving shower gifts on behalf of the school.

Appendix A
Small Group Cards

(Cut out individual letters and laminate for class use.)

A	B
C	D
E	F

Appendix B
Leader Acumen Interpretation Matrix

When reviewing your self/CIRCLE graph, keep in mind there can be four outcomes for each of the five skillsets, as well as your total leader acumen score. Begin by considering your total leader acumen, then move to your category of greatest relative weakness. Remember, a strength overused can become a liability.

Leader Acumen Self-/CIRCLE Assessment Matrix

High Self/High CIRCLE	**Low Self/High CIRCLE**
Most Desirable Orientation	*A Problematic Orientation*
Strong in category and strong Self/CIRCLE congruence suggests that **leader acumen** orientation is well developed and recognized.	(Preferred over a High Self/Low CIRCLE orientation)
Skill enhancement is advisable for continued success.	Low self scores and high CIRCLE scores indicate a **leader acumen** lacking in leader self-confidence.
	Leader growth is needed, although the CIRCLE has confidence in the leader.
High Self/Low CIRCLE	**Low Self/Low CIRCLE**
A Problematic Orientation	*Least Desirable Orientation*
Leadership Potential for Egocentric/Narcissistic Orientation	**Leader acumen** with most room for growth.
Weak CIRCLE congruence suggests a need for leader growth and development of the leader-CIRCLE relationship.	Though there may be congruence between the self and CIRCLE scores in this orientation, this **leader acumen** suggests a need for leader growth and development of the leader-CIRCLE relationship focused on success.
Without growth, derailment is likely.	

The self and CIRCLE scores, as well as congruence of the self and CIRCLE scores, vary along a spectrum from low to high. For each scenario, the Authors' Choices are typical of high self/high CIRCLE responses. This matrix represents the most likely outcomes and orientations.

Appendix C
Leadership Orientation

Being perceived as and feeling individually that you are competent is vital to leader success. To this end, school leaders, like competent leaders in all fields, impact the perceptions of others by the way they behave/act/speak. Those behaviors/acts/utterances exemplify the leader's level of competence to organizational members and constituents. But how can a leader gain insight or come to understand how they are perceived? One way is to gain such insight/understanding into how they are perceived is through 360-evaluative feedback.

In combination with that feedback, it is vital that a leader individually be consistently reflective personally and professionally. That reflective process allows a leader to understand who they are and what they stand for as a leader and defines their leadership competence. That competence is one characteristic that tends to set them apart as a leader, to give them discernibility. And competence is often the key to both long-term and short-term success as a leader.

A list of characteristics often associated with effective leadership in education is provided here. Rate each item below on a scale of 1 to 10 (with 1 being lowest importance and 10 being highest importance) in relation to the item's importance in displaying leadership competence.

1	*Establish principles of treating people*	*1*	*2*	*3*	*4*	*5*	*6*	*7*	*8*	*9*	*10*
2	Foster collaboration	1	2	3	4	5	6	7	8	9	10
3	Seek opportunities to make changes	1	2	3	4	5	6	7	8	9	10
4	Envision the future with a unique image	1	2	3	4	5	6	7	8	9	10
5	Keep hope and determination alive	1	2	3	4	5	6	7	8	9	10
6	Experiment and take risks	1	2	3	4	5	6	7	8	9	10
7	Set standards of excellence	1	2	3	4	5	6	7	8	9	10
8	Get people to see exciting possibilities	1	2	3	4	5	6	7	8	9	10

9	Recognize individuals' contributions	1	2	3	4	5	6	7	8	9	10
10	Build team spirit	1	2	3	4	5	6	7	8	9	10
11	Breathe life into the (organizational) vision	1	2	3	4	5	6	7	8	9	10
12	Share rewards within the team	1	2	3	4	5	6	7	8	9	10
13	Actively involve others	1	2	3	4	5	6	7	8	9	10
14	Create opportunities for success	1	2	3	4	5	6	7	8	9	10
15	Accept mistakes, disappointments, and failures as opportunities to learn	1	2	3	4	5	6	7	8	9	10

Table based on Simon Black, "Qualities of Effective Leadership in Higher Education," *Open Journal of Leadership* 4 (2015): 54–66.

Enter your rating for each item here and in the following scoring rubric for leadership orientation.

1 ___	2 ___	3 ___	4 ___	5 ___
6 ___	7 ___	8 ___	9 ___	10 ___
11 ___	12 ___	13 ___	14 ___	15 ___

Enter your rating in the following scoring grid to find your total scores and subsequently your strengths.

Scoring: Models the Way = sum items 1, 7, and 14

___ + ___ + ___ = _____
  1   7   14   Models the Way total score

Inspire a Shared Vision = sum items 4, 8, and 11

___ + ___ + ___ = _____
  4   8   11   Inspire a Shared Vision total score

Challenge the Process = sum items 3, 6, and 15

___ + ___ + ___ = _____
  3   6   15   Challenge the Process total score

Enable Others to Act = sum items 2, 10, and 13

___ + ___ + ___ = _____
  2   10   13   Enable Others to Act total score

Encourage the Heart = sum items 5, 9, and 12

$$\frac{}{5} + \frac{}{9} + \frac{}{12} = \underline{}$$
Encourage the Heart total score

Interpretation: The scores represent your emphasis of a given orientation as a school leader. The higher the score, the more prominent that orientation emphasis is likely to be in your leadership activities.

Appendix D
Fun at Work?

Happiness is a highly individualized and internalized feeling both personally and professionally. While for purposes of discussion, personal and professional happiness can be separated, the two often carry over and impact each other. Still, being happy in our personal lives does not guarantee happiness in our professional lives, nor does the opposite apply.

Beyond whatever carryover exists, a leader has minimal opportunities to impact the personal happiness of organizational members. Conversely, there are things a leader can do to increase potential professional happiness.

Rate each following item on a scale of 1 to 10 (with 1 being lowest importance and 10 being highest importance) in relation to the item's importance in promoting organizational members' professional happiness. **A scoring rubric is provided.**

A	*Encourage organizational members to offer praise when accomplishments are achieved*	1	2	3	4	5	6	7	8	9	10
B	Provide access to high-quality training and professional growth opportunities	1	2	3	4	5	6	7	8	9	10
C	At appropriate times, encourage staff members to take earned time off	1	2	3	4	5	6	7	8	9	10
D	Display energy and enthusiasm in working with organizational members	1	2	3	4	5	6	7	8	9	10
E	Ensure that pay and benefits are competitive, fair, equal for equal work, and maximized	1	2	3	4	5	6	7	8	9	10
F	Be cordial and friendly	1	2	3	4	5	6	7	8	9	10
G	Provide organizational members opportunities for decision making discretion*	1	2	3	4	5	6	7	8	9	10
H	Offer to mentor aspiring leaders	1	2	3	4	5	6	7	8	9	10

I	Provide feedback about performance	1	2	3	4	5	6	7	8	9	10
J	Have and share an optimistic outlook as a leader	1	2	3	4	5	6	7	8	9	10
K	Provide equal access to opportunities for promotion	1	2	3	4	5	6	7	8	9	10
L	Deflect praise for successes to the responsible organizational members	1	2	3	4	5	6	7	8	9	10

Source: Porath, C., Spreitzer, G., Gibson, C., and Garnett, F. G. "Thriving at Work: Toward Its Measurement, Construct Validation, and Theoretical Refinement." *Journal of Organizational Behavior* 33, no. 2 (2012): 250–75.

Enter your rating in the following scoring grid to find your total scores and subsequently your strengths.

Scoring: Egocentric = sum items D, F, H, and J

$$\underline{} + \underline{} + \underline{} + \underline{} = \underline{}$$
D   F   H   J   Total Egocentric score

People-oriented = sum items A, C, E, and L

$$\underline{} + \underline{} + \underline{} + \underline{} = \underline{}$$
A   C   E   L   Total People-oriented score

Task-oriented = sum items B, G, I, and K

$$\underline{} + \underline{} + \underline{} + \underline{} = \underline{}$$
B   G   I   K   Total Task-oriented score

Interpretation: The scores represent your tendencies toward behaviors that promote organizational member professional happiness. The higher the score, the more prominent this orientation is likely to be in your leadership activities. Maximum score for each category is 40.

Background: Professional satisfaction/happiness has been shown to be related to worker performance. Therefore, incorporating those behaviors in a leader's repertoire of behaviors enhances the probability of worker satisfaction/happiness and organizational productivity.

Appendix E
Self-Knowledge

Warren Bennis, a well-known author and leadership expert, says of leaders, "The ruling quality of leaders, adaptive capacity, is what allows true leaders to make the nimble decisions that bring success. Adaptive capacity is also what allows some people to transcend the setbacks and losses that come with age and to reinvent themselves again and again."[1]

Bennis's notion of adaptive capacity can be viewed as an applied amalgamation of the personality traits espoused in the five-factor model of personality. McCrea and John, in describing the five-factor model, held that there are "five basic dimensions: Extraversion, Agreeableness, Conscientiousness, Neuroticism, and Openness to Experience."[2] Neuroticism, in this instance, can be further defined as emotional stability.

1. Read each item carefully.
2. Select the answer that best describes how often you engage in the behavior described (A) Always (B) Often, (C) Occasionally, (D) Seldom, or (E) Never.
3. Circle the letter (A, B, C, D, or E) of the answer you select.

A scoring rubric is provided after the activity.

Item #	Item	Often	Occasionally	Seldom	Never
A	I like to join multiple groups/organizations.	B	C	D	E
B	I consider myself imaginative in my approach tasks.	B	C	D	E
C	I am even tempered.	B	C	D	E
D	I am hardworking.	B	C	D	E
E	I am generally good natured.	B	C	D	E

F	I am comfortable personally and professionally.	B	C	D	E
G	I have a strong sense of curiosity.	B	C	D	E
H	I am punctual.	B	C	D	E
I	I tend to be forgiving of mistakes.	B	C	D	E
J	I remain calm in most situations.	B	C	D	E
K	I am active physically and mentally.	B	C	D	E
L	I seek new approaches.	B	C	D	E
M	I am trusting of others.	B	C	D	E
N	I am highly verbal.	B	C	D	E
O	I am well organized.	B	C	D	E

Scale items based on the "Examples of Adjectives, Q-Sort Items, and Questionnaire Scales Defining the Five Factors" (McCrae, R. R., and John, O. P., "An Introduction to the Five-Factor Model and Its Applications," *Journal of Personality* 60, no. 2 [1992], 178–79).

SCORING

For the letter selected for each item, give yourself the following points. Then total the scores for each category.
A = 5   B = 4   C = 3   D = 2   E = 1

Total

1. Extraversion   1__   11__   14__   (__)

2. Agreeableness   5__   9__   13__   (__)

3. Conscientiousness   4__   8__   15__   (__)

4. Neuroticism (emotional stability)   3__   6__   10__   (__)

5. Openness to experience   2__   7__   12__   (__)

Interpretation: The wide acceptance of the five-factor model and the extensive research indicating the relationship of the model's factors to leadership and life success make it essential that leaders understand their personality tendencies and dispositions. The results of this scale indicate your self-perception in relation to the aspects five factor model. A higher score in a given area indicates that your personality tends to reflect characteristics of that factor.

Background: The five-factor model of personality has been shown to be related to a variety factors that contribute to leadership success such as job satisfaction,[3] life satisfaction,[4] organization citizenship,[5] and work environment.[6] Aspects of the model, specifically extraversion and agreeableness, have been shown to be positively related to transformational leadership.[7]

Appendix F
Activities to Improve Your Leader Acumen

Now is a good time to reflect on the navigational analysis from *The Soft Skills of Leadership: Navigating with Confidence and Humility*, second edition.[1] Let's consider that you are the driver for a chartered bus with thirty-five travelers to a landmark tourist adventure six hundred miles away.

You have made many trips over your life that were six hundred miles or longer, but perhaps you have never been to this particular destination. Maybe some of those on the bus are older than you are and have driven longer. Perhaps, even, some of them have been to the destination at hand on a previous occasion. Prior to embarking on the trip, you have several options in preparation for the trip.

Regardless of how you choose to prepare, each of your travelers has their own expectations regarding the trip. Some may wish you would drive faster; others might wish you would have taken the more leisurely scenic route. Still others may question the detours, pit stops, and even announcements you make. All of these factors (and many others) would inform their feedback on your performance as a driver.

After returning from your destination and having a little time to reflect on the trip, you, too, might consider different decisions you would make if you had the chance to drive the bus again. Your own reflections as well as the passengers' feedback would certainly leave an imprint. How strong an imprint might depend on the degree of congruence between your perception of the trip and theirs.

In order to improve the next trip (not to imply that this one was a bad one), the driver needs to be reflective, ask for feedback, and plan for the future. This planning (for improvement) could include a myriad of things from using a more updated map (or GPS) to planning to take the trip at a better time of year. It will include both study and action.

The same planning for improvement, study, and action is true with leader acumen. The scenarios in the field book are given to help the leader consider the myriad of solutions to different problems and to become more effective and efficient at resolving them. Whether in a group setting—with the rich dialogue, discourse, and reflective dynamics that setting generates—or considered individually, study leading to action will be the best teacher and provide a clear/direct route to success in increasing your leader acumen.

As the leader becomes aware of and chooses the leader acumen imperative (credibility, competence, inspiration, vision, or emotional intelligence) they would most like to improve, along with the exercises in the book, the following activities are recommended. For the best results, these activities should be planned and acted upon over a period of not less than six months.

To improve your credibility, while working through the book scenarios, as odd as it may seem, write an article or research paper for publication to share your experiences and expertise. This is *not* a one-week assignment. You should set aside (at a minimum) weekly time to work on the article or paper: organizing, researching, and writing the article or paper. This won't just be for the sake of obtaining facts and information; it will also be for the purpose of presenting them. How you present yourself in your writing is a huge part of your credibility.

If you rush through and/or are sloppy, you leave a distinctly poor impression with the reader (think emails, memoranda, and even handwritten notes). As a leader, in any written correspondence, if you give the facts and figures without ensuring they are valid, reliable, and in fact real, again, you lose credibility. As you are preparing your paper, work to triangulate (using multiple data sources) to ensure your credibility. A second option would be to undertake case study readings about historical or contemporary figures you admire and believe to be credible and reflect on what about that individual/those individuals made them credible. These case studies could also be incorporated into your article or research paper.

To improve your competence, while working through the book scenarios, align yourself with a mentor in your field of leadership and meet with them regularly. Try to find opportunities not only to interact with this person on an informal basis, but more importantly find opportunities to shadow this person.

Write down a list of questions to ask about how they arrived at a specific solution or why they took a certain position. Take the time to discuss with your mentor other solutions they (or you) might have considered. Talk to this person about typical problems/issues they encounter and how they approach resolving those problems/issues. Spend as much time talking about the why as the what, how, and about the timing of their decisions. Don't be timid when asking about technical matters. Technical matters form the basis, "the what," people are to accomplish.

To improve your ability to inspire others, while working through the book scenarios, join a speaker's bureau. Conversely, become a coach/sponsor/leader for a children's athletic, drama, music, or scout group. You might rather choose to join adult groups such as a neighborhood watch, owners' association, or a civic group such as Rotary or Lions where you would have the opportunity to lead by your words and actions.

As a member of a speakers' group, seek opportunities to present motivational/inspirational messages regularly. The same is true if you choose to become a volunteer coach/sponsor/leader of children's groups. Be sure that you give motivational pitches regularly to the children. With adults, volunteer to lead or participate in group activities. Being actively involved in the suggested activities should present ample opportunities to both observe and be a part of inspirational activities and should have a corresponding positive impact on your overall ability in this area.

To improve your vision, while working through the book scenarios, embark on a personal improvement plan. This can be anything from a physical, spiritual, mental, or emotional area of your life. This idea is to choose an area for self-improvement and then to map out a six-month plan to reach a specific goal.

As Covey would say, "begin with the end in mind."[2] Once you have created the plan—and it is very detailed and specific—enact the plan. At the end of each month, evaluate and reflect on your progress, and then adjust your plan accordingly. Or, as an alternative strategy, plan an event or series of events for your family or other group with which you are associated. Be sure to engage family or group members in the planning processes to produce a shared vision regarding each event.

The personal plan or the planning of events should engage you actively in the give and take of reaching a personal decision that impacts your individual plan (or the consensus) that is needed for visionary action.

To improve your emotional intelligence/social skills, while working through the book scenarios, commit yourself to involvement with a charitable, civic, school, religious, or other worthwhile organization that is not a part of your work. Focus your energies not only on the betterment of the cause/organization, but specifically on the people affiliated with the cause/organization. Be intentional in your desire to encourage, support, and embolden them.

Or, as an alternative strategy, volunteer to assist in projects sponsored by local civic groups that involve working with people in need or volunteer to work in an appropriate capacity at a hospital or nursing home, or to assist youth groups in your community. The emotional impact of serving others selflessly should provide opportunities for growth in your emotional intelligence.

The combination of intense review of situational judgment tests along with the activities as briefly described here over a period of time will ensure growth in your chosen leader acumen skillset. Not only will your skillset scores improve, but more importantly, your leadership capacity will improve. Your road to success as a leader will be like an up-to-date GPS with all the latest features, newest maps, and best route guidance available.

Notes

PREFACE

1. Warren G. Bennis and Robert Thomas, *Geeks and Geezers: How Era, Values, and Defining Moments Shape Leaders* (Boston, MA: Harvard Business School Publishing, 2002).

2. Ibid.

3. Warren G. Bennis, "The Seven Ages of the Leader," *Harvard Business Review* 82, no. 1 (2004): 46.

4. Dan Harrison, "Leaders Must Exhibit Adaptive Capacity in 2022," (2022), https://hrdailyadvisor.blr.com/2022/02/02/leaders-must-exhibit-adaptive-capacity-in-2022.

5. Ben Ramalingam, David Nabarro, Arkebe Oqubuy, Dame Ruth Carnall, and Leni Wild, "Five Principles to Guide Adaptive Leadership," *Harvard Business Review Digital Articles* 2-6 (2020): 1.

6. Ibid, 2–5.

7. Paul Schoemaker and George Day, "Preparing Organizations for Greater Turbulence," *California Management Review* 63, no. 4 (2021): 66.

8. Antonio Fernandez and Graham Shaw, "Academic Leadership in a Time of Crisis: The Coronavirus and COVID-19," *Journal of Leadership Studies* 14, no. 1 (2020): 44.

9. *Achieving the Dream*, "Building Adaptive Capacity for Resiliency and Agility: A Guide," (2020), https://achievingthedream.org/adaptive-capacity-for-resiliency.

10. Helen Goode, Rachel McGennisken, and Emma Rutherford, "An Adaptive Leadership Response to Unprecedented Change," *International Studies in Educational Administration* 49, no. 1 (2021): 41.

11. Ryan Dunn, "Adaptive Leadership: Leading Through Complexity," *International Studies in Educational Administration* 48, no. 1 (2020): 33.

12. Ibid.

13. Ahmad Nurabadi, Fendy Suhariadi, Antun Mardiyanta, Teguh Triwiyanto, and Maulana Adha, "Digital Principal Instructional Leadership in a New Normal Era," *International Journal of Evaluation and Research in Education* (2022): 1095.

INTRODUCTION

1. Wanda M. Green and Edward E. Leonard, *The Soft Skills of Leadership: Navigating with Confidence and Humility*, second edition (Lanham, MD: Rowman & Littlefield, 2019).
2. Ibid.
3. Disclaimer: At the end of the book are the contributing author's recommended solutions, rationale, and reasoning for rejection of alternative solutions. These recommendations are in no way intended to supersede work policy or act as legal advice to the learner. If encountering similar situations, you should consult with proper authorities and/or act as you deem appropriate based on your own judgment.
The situational judgment test (SJT) scenarios included are based on actual situations encountered by the contributing authors including the solutions they enacted at the time and place of the circumstance and may or may not be appropriate today individually or in your place of work.
4. Wanda M. Green and Edward E. Leonard, *The Soft Skills of Leadership: Navigating with Confidence and Humility*, second edition (Lanham, MD: Rowman & Littlefield, 2019).
5. Ibid.

CHAPTER 1

1. Michael McDaniel and Deborah Whetzel, "Situational Judgement Tests," lecture, IPMAAC Workshop, June 20, 2005.
2. Michael McDaniel, Frederick Morgeson, Elizabeth Finnigan, and Michael Campion, "Use of Situational Judgment Tests to Predict Job Performance: A Clarification of the Literature," *Journal of Applied Psychology* 84, no. 4 (2002): 730–40.
3. Wanda M. Green and Edward E. Leonard, *The Soft Skills of Leadership: Navigating with Confidence and Humility*, second edition (Lanham, MD: Rowman & Littlefield, 2019).
4. Ibid.

CHAPTER 2

1. Wanda M. Green and Edward E. Leonard, *The Soft Skills of Leadership: Navigating with Confidence and Humility*, second edition (Lanham, MD: Rowman & Littlefield, 2019).
2. Christopher Marquis and Andras Tilcsik, "Imprinting: Toward a Multilevel Theory," *The Academy of Management Annals* 7, no. 1 (2013): 195–245.

CHAPTER 3

1. Wanda M. Green and Edward E. Leonard, *The Soft Skills of Leadership: Navigating with Confidence and Humility*, second edition (Lanham, MD: Rowman & Littlefield, 2019).
2. Christopher Marquis and Andras Tilcsik, "Imprinting: Toward a Multilevel Theory," *The Academy of Management Annals* 7, no. 1 (2013): 195–245.
3. Wanda M. Green and Edward E. Leonard, *The Soft Skills of Leadership: Navigating with Confidence and Humility*, second edition (Lanham, MD: Rowman & Littlefield, 2019).

CHAPTER 4

1. Wanda M. Green and Edward E. Leonard, *The Soft Skills of Leadership: Navigating with Confidence and Humility*, second edition (Lanham, MD: Rowman & Littlefield, 2019).
2. Christopher Marquis and Andras Tilcsik, "Imprinting: Toward a Multilevel Theory," *The Academy of Management Annals* 7, no. 1 (2013): 195–245.
3. Wanda M. Green and Edward E. Leonard, *Leadership Intelligence: Navigating to Your True North* (Lanham, MD: Rowman & Littlefield, 2016), 63.

CHAPTER 5

1. Wanda M. Green and Edward E. Leonard, *The Soft Skills of Leadership: Navigating with Confidence and Humility*, second edition (Lanham, MD: Rowman & Littlefield, 2019).
2. Ibid.
3. Christopher Marquis and Andras Tilcsik, "Imprinting: Toward a Multilevel Theory," *The Academy of Management Annals* 7, no. 1 (2013): 195–245.
4. Wanda S. Maulding Green and Edward E. Leonard, *Improving Your Leadership Intelligence: A Field Book for K–12 Leaders* (Lanham, MD: Rowman & Littlefield, 2019), 73.

CHAPTER 6

1. Wanda M. Green and Edward E. Leonard, *The Soft Skills of Leadership: Navigating with Confidence and Humility*, second edition (Lanham, MD: Rowman & Littlefield, 2019).
2. Christopher Marquis and Andras Tilcsik, "Imprinting: Toward a Multilevel Theory," *The Academy of Management Annals* 7, no. 1 (2013): 195–245.

CHAPTER 7

1. In this scenario, Trey is a family friend but policy trumps friendship. You must look out for the best interest of all students and families districtwide. Two years prior to this as a district employee, Trey had the opportunity to voice his concerns on the policy change but chose not to because he didn't think it would affect him or his family. As superintendent, I did agree at the end of the meeting to review the policy at the end of the school year with each school counselor and take it to the board if we felt a change was needed. I would not change or request a change in the middle of the school year.

2. Author's note: The principal immediately hung up with the teacher and contacted her superintendent. After speaking with him, she contacted the sheriff's office and related the events. She then returned the call to her teacher and assured her the matter would be properly handled by authorities with law enforcement officials on campus the next day for extra safety and support. She called a faculty meeting the next morning prior to school and explained what had happened the night before. However, she asked faculty to keep classes as normal as possible. Before buses arrived on campus, the Federal Bureau of Investigation had traced the message to another state where the cousin of a student lived and had sent the message. This person was arrested.

3. As an aside, the aggressor's mother protested vehemently about her son's discipline and made an official complaint against the administrator. Do the right thing even in the face of adversity.

APPENDIX E

1. Warren G. Bennis, "The Seven Ages of the Leader," *Harvard Business Review* 82, no. 1 (2004): 46.

2. R. R. McCrae and O. P. John, "An Introduction to the Five-Factor Model and Its Applications," *Journal of Personality* 60, no. 2 (1992): 175–215.

3. T. A. Judge, D. Heller, and M. K. Mount, "Five-Factor Model of Personality and Job Satisfaction: A Meta-analysis," *Journal of Applied Psychology* 87, no. 3 (2002): 530–41.

4. K. M. DeNeve and H. Cooper, "The Happy Personality: A Meta-analysis of 137 Personality Traits and Subjective Well-being," *Psychological Bulletin* 2 (1998): 197.

5. D. S. Chiaburu, I. Oh, C. M. Berry, N. Li, and R. G. Gardner, "The Five-Factor Model of Personality Traits and Organizational Citizenship Behaviors: A Meta-analysis," *The Journal of Applied Psychology* 96, no. 6 (2011): 1140–66.

6. J. A. Ruth, "An Examination of the Impact of the Big Five Personality Traits and Work Environment on the Leadership Behaviors of Millennial Generation Employees," *Dissertation Abstracts International Section A* 76 (2016).

7. T. A. Judge and J. E. Bono, "Five-Factor Model of Personality and Transformational Leadership," *Journal of Applied Psychology* 85, no. 5 (2000): 751–65.

APPENDIX F

1. Wanda M. Green and Edward E. Leonard, *The Soft Skills of Leadership: Navigating with Confidence and Humility*, second edition (Lanham, MD: Rowman & Littlefield, 2019).

2. Stephen R. Covey, *The 7 Habits of Highly Effective People: Powerful Lessons in Personal Change* (New York: Simon & Schuster, 2020).

www.ingramcontent.com/pod-product-compliance
Lightning Source LLC
Chambersburg PA
CBHW030403170426
43202CB00010B/1468